AVEN
AS
ON'S
S IT

3

4

7

KODAK 5063 TX

8 ▷ 18A 11 1

10

12

BOBBI, WHEN YOU HAVE HARD TIMES, SOMETIMES IT TEACHES YOU WHAT TO DO

Aunt Alice

16

17

15

18

Still Bobbi

Still Bobbi

BOBBI BROWN

**MARYSUE
RUCCI
BOOKS**

New York Amsterdam/Antwerp London
Toronto Sydney/Melbourne New Delhi

MARYSUE
RUCCI
BOOKS

An Imprint of Simon & Schuster, LLC
1230 Avenue of the Americas
New York, NY 10020

First Marysue Rucci Books hardcover edition September 2025

MARYSUE RUCCI BOOKS and colophon are trademarks of Simon & Schuster, LLC

Simon & Schuster strongly believes in freedom of expression and stands against
censorship in all its forms. For more information, visit BooksBelong.com.

For information about special discounts for bulk purchases, please contact Simon & Schuster
Special Sales at 1-866-506-1949 or business@simonandschuster.com.

The Simon & Schuster Speakers Bureau can bring authors to your live event.
For more information or to book an event, contact the Simon & Schuster Speakers
Bureau at 1-866-248-3049 or visit our website at www.simonspeakers.com.

INTERIOR DESIGN BY KARLA SCHWEER

Manufactured in the United States of America

1 3 5 7 9 10 8 6 4 2

Library of Congress Cataloging-in-Publication Data has been applied for
ISBN 978-1-6680-8217-1
ISBN 978-1-6680-8219-5 (ebook)

TO STEVEN, THE LOVE OF MY LIFE.

CONTENTS

Still Bobbi

"I WON'T WANT TO WORK WHEN I'M SIXTY."

The year was 1995, and I was sitting with my husband, Steven, at our dining room table, ready to sign the biggest contract of my life.

Bobbi Brown Cosmetics, the little makeup company we founded in 1991, had been outselling the giant corporations, and it didn't take long for one of those giants—Estée Lauder—to approach us with an eye-popping offer. There was only one catch: as part of the deal, I couldn't start another competing company for twenty-five years.

Steven gave me a wary look as my pen hovered over the dotted line. "Are you sure?" he said.

I did the math on my fingers. I was thirty-seven years old. In twenty-five years, I'd be . . . thirty-eight, thirty-nine, forty . . . sixty-two! Time to retire! Pour me a tequila shot!

I turned to Steven and uttered those famous last words: I won't want to work when I'm sixty.

Fast-forward twenty-one years, to 2016, when things got complicated at Estée Lauder and I left with four and a half years remaining on my non-compete. At fifty-nine years old, I could retire. My kids were out of the house. I never needed to work again. Most people would have taken a year off, gone to Paris, learned to play tennis. I gave it some thought, but none of that interested me. I never had hobbies. For the last twenty-five years, I'd been working building a business, and when I wasn't working, I had three hungry boys to feed, PTA meetings and baseball games to attend, a sink full of dishes to wash, and a pile of kids' sneakers to tidy. Those were my hobbies. On the precious few occasions when all that work was done, you'd find me picking out paints to redecorate the kitchen, or new throw pillows for the couch. My mind loves creative work. In fact, it's not even work. It's a passion.

There I was, at sixty, with no demands on my time and nothing but time to spare. I still felt that same creative passion, but where could I put it?

After climbing my way up from a struggling freelance makeup artist to having created a billion-dollar company, what comes next?

PART ONE

KNOW WHERE YOU'RE FROM

CHAPTER ONE

NANA AND PAPA

At the age of fourteen my grandfather Papa Sam sailed from Ukraine to America, alone.

Imagine leaving your home as a child, saying goodbye to all that is familiar and comforting, and traveling across the world to a place where you don't speak the language and everyone is a stranger. He must have suffered lonely nights missing home, but he didn't wallow. Wallowing was a luxury he couldn't afford. He got on with it.

At first he hawked newspapers on the city streets to well-heeled

Chicagoans. Then he sold ladies' handbags downtown. For a struggling immigrant, there was no such thing as a career. He took whatever jobs made money, whatever jobs put a warm meal in his stomach. But he was always searching for the next step up, the next opportunity to become something better.

He scrimped and eventually saved enough money to buy a gas station. One day, someone abandoned a car there. When he was sure the owner was never coming back, Papa Sam sold the car for three hundred dollars, and a new career was born. Across the street from the gas station stood an empty store next to a restaurant. He went into the restaurant and said, "Someone is going to open a competing restaurant next to you and drive you out of business, but if you lend me two thousand dollars, I'll open a car dealership instead." That's how he became a car dealer, selling cars to nice suburban families and to infamous gangsters like Al Capone and Meyer Lansky.

Papa Sam met my grandmother Hermina (everyone called her Minnie) at a party in Chicago in the late 1920s. The details are lost to time, but I can imagine what it must have been like: the fashion, the makeup, the music. They made quite a couple. He was a little five-foot-five man who dressed impeccably and talked with a tough guy's Chicago accent. She was a tiny woman who never raised her voice and who loved her family ferociously.

Both Nana and Papa were incredibly hard working and very old-fashioned. Papa was the head of the family, no question about it. Nana's whole life was Papa and her children—and later, her grand-children. She never attended college, and never had a job. She came from an era when a woman handled the domestic responsibilities, and she did it happily. Papa usually worked late, and Nana waited for him to come home before serving dinner. The second he opened the front door, it was all about him.

Soon after they married, Nana and Papa welcomed their first daughter, Alice. Six years later came my mother, Sandra. It was the depths of the Great Depression, but Papa Sam had a special ability to survive and flourish. He sold enough cars to keep his family afloat and to spoil my mother like crazy—according to my Aunt Alice, the eldest child, who swears she never got the same treatment. Papa Sam even named his car dealership Sandra Motors, after my mother, so enthralled was he by his baby girl.

By the 1950s, Papa Sam was called "Cadillac Sam" and had built one of the biggest car dealerships in Chicago. He was proud of his business, and proud of the radio and TV commercials he starred in. Everywhere he went, whether a sandwich shop, a clothing store, or the fruit market in Skokie, everyone treated him like a king. He loved being a big shot. He'd go to the same restaurants, a five-dollar bill folded in his hand for the maître d', and push open the doors to the refrain: "Sam! You're here!" A waiter would then show him to his table and plug in a phone at Papa's booth in case he needed to make a call.

As a local businessman of note, he was selected to meet Harry Truman during a presidential visit to Chicago in the 1940s. Imagine the transformation: the immigrant boy who spoke no English to the businessman deemed worthy to meet the president of the United States. It must have blown his mind. Sadly, he died in 1996, long before President Obama appointed me to the US International Trade Commission. Whenever President Obama would see me, he'd say

"Hey, B-Squared, what's going on?" and I'd think of Papa. He would have been so proud.

When Papa Sam was pushing eighty, he was convinced to retire. Who wants to work when they're eighty? Well, as it turned out, Papa Sam did. He didn't have hobbies (I guess I got that from him). All he knew was work. Without his work, he became depressed. His life, his purpose, was providing for his family. So, he unretired. He had a promotional brochure printed and sent to his old customers. It featured a picture of him holding his great-grandson (my oldest son, Dylan, six months old). The caption read: "I tried to retire, and I didn't like it. So I'm back and I have a deal for you."

What made me think I would want to retire at sixty?

CHAPTER TWO

MEET THE BROWNS

My mother was the most glamorous woman I have ever known. To me, she looked like a young Jackie Kennedy. She was five foot two and always wore high heels to gain a couple extra inches. As a child, she struggled with her weight, so when she lost it later in life, she loved to show off in the tightest clothes she could find, emphasizing her tiny waist. I never saw her without impeccable makeup, hair, and outfit. As a child, I'd stare at her as she stood in front of the mirror and made up her face, her lit cigarette hanging off the edge of the counter. I watched the way her delicate fingers grasped her charcoal eyebrow pencil as she carefully filled in her eyebrows. With a toothpick she'd put on her false eyelashes, then rub bronzer on her cheeks and uncap one of her lipstick tubes to apply a pale lip. That's how I fell in love with makeup and beauty.

At a college party, my mom met my dad, James (Joe) Brown, and fell in love. They were two very young beautiful people who also happened to share the experience of being chubby kids. My dad's nickname growing up was Fat Boy, but when he lost all the weight in high school, he looked like a young Michael Landon. He had piercing blue eyes that could light up a room. My girlfriends were obsessed with him. They called him Gorge, as in "gorgeous," and they'd come over just to get a look at him. Still, he always had that old nickname in the back of his head. As a result, he too put great importance on appearances.

My parents were loving, wonderful people. When I was born in 1957, they were only twenty-one and twenty-two years old. Brother Michael came about three years later, and Linda, who was my little doll, came two and a half years after that, which meant my parents had three kids by the time they were in their mid-twenties. No one thought twice about such a thing back then.

They dealt with that pressure in different ways. My dad, a brilliant, well-read, successful lawyer, wanted to be original, to break out of the mold. His law practice gave him a steady salary, but it wasn't his passion. During my childhood, he tried to reinvent himself several times. He loved writing, so he first pivoted from law to work as a magazine travel writer. They sent him to Croatia and other far-off places. He pivoted from that and became a day trader, then he started a junket business, where he'd take gamblers on a private plane to the Bahamas or Las Vegas. That was fun because he often took Michael, Linda, and me with him. He was chasing his dreams, but he realized he couldn't support us with these jobs, so he reopened his law practice. Watching him, I realized that life could be more exciting than working an unfulfilling job. I learned that I could chase and fulfill my passion. I knew he wanted that for me too.

Later in life, I found a manuscript my dad had written about a New York City taxi driver named Marceau who teaches the world about imagination and curiosity. As a gift for my dad's seventieth birthday, I had a friend at Scholastic print one hundred books, and on a trip, I put them in a bookstore window in Telluride, Colorado. We walked by on the way to dinner, and upon seeing his own book there, he was floored. We went inside so he could take it all in. He could not stop talking about what a gift it was. We later went on a press tour together in New York City—including a spot on the *Today* show with Al Roker and book signings with Ann Curry. Dad ended up retiring early, walking away from his law practice and becoming a full-time children's book author. Scholastic edited and reprinted his first book and updated it with art he had commissioned. He has now written ten books, many of them self-published. At age ninety, he still reads in classrooms and teaches the power of imagination. Lesson learned: passion and work are a winning combination.

My mom tried hard to make me feel special and I absolutely adored her. When I was little, she was always there when I needed her. And as I grew older, she loved sharing her beauty rituals with me. She'd take me to Woolworth once a week and buy a big tub of Queen Helene clay mask, which we'd take home and rub on our faces for an at-home spa night. Waiting for the mask to work its magic, we'd do manicures and pedicures, then we'd wash off the mask and moisturize, moisturize, moisturize. In later years, sometimes she'd wax my legs and my bikini line. She was very practical. Yes, we could have gone to the salon, but why not do it at home? I'd lie on the kitchen table, and she'd set newspapers down and get to work.

On occasion, my mom let me skip school. She'd pull her credit card out and say, "Charge it!" and we'd go running out the door on a shopping spree. If I saw something I liked, she wanted me to get it in three colors. My dad made enough money at his law practice so that we were comfortably upper-middle class, but we certainly weren't rich. I didn't take these extravagances for granted.

My mother needed to be the perfect wife, the perfect house-keeper, the perfect mother. Maybe as a result, I felt I needed to be perfect for her.

My mother's perfectionism in the house might explain why I'm a little nutty to this day with visual order. I can walk into any room and immediately find what's wrong with it. I've learned this ability does not always endear you to others, but I came by it honestly. My mother inspected our bedrooms every Monday after school. She wanted the clothes folded in the drawers like she had folded them when she put the laundry away. Dirty clothes needed to be in a hamper. Everything had a place. And if things weren't in pristine order, we couldn't leave the house until we'd fixed what was wrong. Early on, I learned to keep my room clean so I could go out to play. I guess I always had a practical mind.

When I was in middle school my mom started to act different—a little sad, a bit paranoid. Just off. She could be biting about my looks and my weight. Until then I'd experienced a warm and caring mother most of the time. But she had such high standards. I wanted to be perfect as a result. I remember feeling I wasn't good enough, smart enough, thin enough, or pretty enough for her.

It soon became clear my mom was struggling with mental illness. And when she got sick, things could turn dark, fast. She tried to take her life several times. Once, she jumped out of a car while she was driving. The car swerved out of control and brought down a streetlamp before ending up totaled on the side of the road. My mother walked away with a broken fingernail, and missing a heel on her shoe. We later learned she was bipolar, but she had to live through an era when no one talked about mental health and there was limited understanding of it, let alone help in dealing with such things.

I was thirteen when my mother had her first nervous breakdown and ended up in a hospital for a few months. My dad hired a woman to come in and create a semblance of stability for us. She'd make hamburgers for dinner, put the buns on the grill and slather them with mayonnaise. Bread and mayo! My mother would have never allowed that. It was a huge treat in a hard time. After dinner, Dad and I would drive to visit Mom, just the two of us. Michael, at ten years old, and Linda, at eight, were too young. Driving half an hour to the locked hospital ward downtown gave me and my dad a chance to bond. He'd pop in the 8-track, and we'd listen to rock music—he loved Creedence Clearwater Revival—while we talked about school, my brother, my sister, my mom.

One of the best things about each of my parents was that I could talk to them. When my mom was healthy, I shared things with her that most kids would never tell their mom. The first time I smoked pot as a teenager, I came home and said, "Guess what I just did?" She didn't punish, judge, or lecture me. She just told me to be careful.

I felt equally comfortable with my dad. Having those heart-to-heart moments with him while driving to see my mom made me feel pretty grown up, but I was still a child dealing with things that were too heavy for me to understand.

At the hospital, my mom was usually quiet and depressed. They gave her lithium, which numbed her. She spent most of her time making ashtrays and crocheting napkins. Seeing her like that was difficult and heartbreaking, but the scariest part was seeing the other patients walking around making all kinds of noises. It was like a scene from *One Flew Over the Cuckoo's Nest*. My mother got better, but she always struggled. She ended up in the hospital several more times during my childhood.

When things got tough at home, Nana and Papa's house became my sanctuary. They lived thirty minutes away in the city. I'd often be with Nana in the evening, waiting for Papa to come home from work. Then we'd sit around the table listening to stories from his day while Nana served him dinner. After dinner, we would stuff envelopes full of brochures and advertisements for his car dealership and lick the stamps for him to mail out the next day.

I grew up watching the way Papa did business, the way he treated his salesmen, his mechanics, his customers—many had been with him for decades—and even strangers off the street. One time a man came into the dealership carrying a big shopping bag. He looked rough, possibly homeless. None of the sales guys would go near him, but Papa Sam put his arm around the man and said, "How ya doing, boss?" Turns out the shopping bag was full of cash, and the man bought two cars that day.

These were invaluable lessons to me. They gave me an entrepreneurial mindset from an early age. When I was about twelve years old, my friends and I started a jewelry store called LBJ (Lynn, Bobbi, and Janice). Our headquarters were in my parents' basement. We'd make little bracelets and necklaces, put them on display, and wait for customers to arrive. I'm not sure what customers we were expecting in the basement. Nevertheless, it was an early attempt to do what Papa Sam did.

Papa and Nana always made me feel important. When I think of Nana, I think of rose perfume and unconditional love. She loved the essence of me. She made it okay to be myself. In my house, there were rules. With Nana, the rules were relaxed. She loved to spoil me at the soda shop. She'd buy me pretzels and ice cream floats, and tip the soda jockey enough that he remembered her name. After a few trips with Nana, he remembered my name too. It felt special to be included in her world.

Papa wasn't as quick to spoil me as Nana was, but it didn't take much to get past his gruff exterior to the mush inside. He once let me, Michael, and Linda dress him up in girls' clothes and makeup. We made him wear high heels and walk around the room while we howled with laughter. He loved us so much, he'd let us do whatever we wanted.

This powerful, loving connection helped me navigate my home life. After my mom's first breakdown, my dad checked out of the marriage. I'm sure it was tough for him. He had to work full time, support my mother, and deal with three kids at home. I think he did a phenomenal job, but it was just too much.

The summer after eighth grade, I learned my parents were getting divorced. During a trip to my grandparents' lake house in Michiana, my parents took us all for a walk. As my brother and sister trailed behind us out of earshot, my mother and father held hands and said, "Bobbi, can we talk to you? We just want to tell you, we're getting a divorce." I was flabbergasted. I never even heard them fighting. I didn't know anyone who was divorced.

I don't remember much of what came next. I'm sure I was sad, and I knew I had to put on a good face and a good front for my brother and sister. But mostly, I accepted it. Besides, I had reached the age when nothing is more important than your friends.

By the time my parents decided to divorce, my mom was healthy enough to take custody of us kids. Dad remained in our lives, but it was a bumpy transition. On our first outing alone with him, he took us to a Cubs game, with seats near the field. I was having a great time until a foul ball came and smacked me in the head. The second visit, my dad took us to see a cousin in Wisconsin. This guy raised animals in his backyard, including caged lions and tigers. My sister petted a lion on his nose between the bars of the cage, and it chomped down on her hand. My dad slammed his body against the cage and the lion opened its jaws to show my sister's finger dangling by a thread of skin. Luckily, they reattached it at the hospital.

Meanwhile, my mother's hairdresser introduced her to his ex-father-in-law, Norty, and they fell madly in love. My mother was incredibly happy with Norty. He offered her stability, which she needed. They got married, and all of a sudden, our house was a zoo. He had three kids of his own: a daughter, who was seven or eight years older than me, a son my age, and another son the same age as Michael. It wasn't easy, but my mother handled it well. She loved the commotion. So did I. I thought it was fun. I guess I've always been the type to love a bustling, busy house. Sadly, Norty was not in our lives for very long: he died of a heart attack when I was in college. The trauma caused my mother to relapse and she had to be hospitalized again to treat her depression. In later years, one stepbrother, with whom I was very close, died of AIDS, and I drifted apart from the other stepsiblings.

Growing up amid such tumult was harder on my siblings than it was on me. Michael was the most beautiful boy. He inherited my dad's brains and good looks, whereas I did not. Michael never studied but still aced every test. Unfortunately, I think he might have inherited my mother's mental illness too. He was always troubled and usually in trouble. At age sixteen, he took my father's car and wrapped it around a tree. The hospital called and said, "You'd better call your priest because he's not going to make it." He was in a coma and had a halo brace on his neck. My mother nursed him back to health. They were codependent. She would literally do anything for him, and she did.

Michael was diagnosed early in adulthood with borderline personality disorder, a terrible illness because there is no medicine to treat it. Unlike my mother, who eventually controlled her bipolar disorder with medication, Michael didn't stand a chance. He tried to self-medicate: something to wake up, something to focus, and something to go to bed. Later in life, I tried to support him as much as I could, but it never worked. He died at sixty years old of a drug overdose.

My baby sister, Linda, is my best friend. She's a very special soul and was born with a happy gene. She can't help but see the world in a positive light. I think she took the pain of those early years and turned it into a dedication to help others. She's worked as a special-ed teacher, a massage therapist, a Pilates instructor, and a health coach. In addition to raising three children of her own, she took care of our mother until my Mom died in 2023, and is now doing the same for our father.

As for me, even during the hardest of those teenage years, I was developing an emotional resilience that has carried me through my life. Believe me, I felt the sadness, pain, and fear of my mother's illness and my brother's difficulties—even today if I dwell too much on what happened to them, I feel the pain in my gut. Same with my parents' divorce. These things affected me. But I somehow got through them. I didn't block them out, but I also didn't let them hold me back. I moved forward. I'm not exactly sure how I learned or earned this ability. But I've learned what works for me is to share what I'm feeling with my close family and friends, so I can process my emotions and not have the hardships take over my life.

CHAPTER THREE

AUNT ALICE SENSE

Then there's Aunt Alice.

I adored my mom and was proud that she was my mother, but I often felt more like Aunt Alice's daughter than my mother's daughter. Aunt Alice didn't care about the same things my mother did. She kept her hair short, didn't wear a lot of makeup, and wore flat shoes and comfortable clothes. At my house we talked about appearances. At her house we talked about life. My house was the perfect shoes. Her house was the fuzzy slippers. These two forces—glamorous mom and practical Aunt Alice—sowed the seeds for the invention of no-makeup makeup, and my career.

Aunt Alice lived just down the road, and I was there a lot. It was joy from the second you walked in: music downstairs, people jumping in the pool, a table full of snacks. We'd go swimming, and then I'd put on one of her handmade towel robes, and we'd sit around with a big bowl of ice cream watching television. I could never eat a bowl of ice cream in my own house. Everything at Aunt Alice's was about being comfortable in your own skin.

If she was like a second mother to me, her daughter Barbara was like a sister. Being around them gave me a sense of stability, especially during my parents' divorce. When I was having a tough time, I would go over to Aunt Alice's and everything would disappear.

In a more subtle way, Aunt Alice also influenced my marriage—or at least my idea of what marriage could be. I was lucky enough to watch her love affair with Uncle Albert, which lasted more than sixty years. They reminded me of Paul Newman and Joanne Woodward. They were so close, you never saw Al without Alice. Like Papa Sam, Uncle Al had a dealership, with sixty-eight employees spread across three locations. This allowed Aunt Alice to work with him while her kids were in school and still come home at two thirty and put an apron on, and her kids would never know she was gone. When Uncle Al died, the rabbi at his funeral said, "I usually give a eulogy, but today I'm going to tell a love story."

Through the years, Aunt Alice and I have grown even closer. Our conversations are filled with common sense advice, and she often settles me down and gives me a fresh perspective on whatever it is I'm complaining about. She's also been an inspiration at work. I've made and named many beauty products in her honor, from lipstick to perfume. I even named one lipstick Party Alice.

Now in her nineties, Aunt Alice remains the embodiment of my concept that natural and comfortable is beautiful. She is strong, funny, and brilliant. She has more common sense than anyone I have ever met. When she says, "Look . . ." I pay attention, because I know I'm going to get some major advice. She is relentlessly positive. Her eyes light up when she talks about how happy she is, even after losing the love of her life. She taught me that it's what you do after the hard times that makes you strong. I value her advice so much, I even started a series when I was beauty editor at Yahoo called "Ask Aunt Alice," where we got a chance to share her wisdom with the world.

A few choice nuggets:

Plastic surgery: "I would never do it. I had one friend who did her neck, it cost her thirteen thousand dollars, she said it was the most painful thing she'd ever done, and a few years later, it all fell down."

Makeup: "Very little."

Beauty philosophy: "It's nice to put makeup on, but I think everybody is beautiful. Everybody has something about them that's beautiful. Inner beauty is so important."

Beauty advice: "Keep your face clean and moisturize."

Health: "Too many people look for the magic pill."

Happiness: "I've always seen the cup as half-full. If you're unhappy, find out what's causing it and see if you can do something about it. Aside from illness, there's nothing you can't find a way to fix."

That's Aunt Alice. As a result, it's also very much me. Her outlook on life influenced me as a child. It stuck with me as a young adult. It set the tone for my work as a makeup artist and brand creator, as well as a wife and mother. It still guides me today.

CHAPTER FOUR

KNOW WHERE YOU'RE FROM

This is where I come from. Good and bad, these influences made me what I am. My parents: two wonderful, loving, and complex people obsessed with beauty, health, and body image who taught me I could be anything. It makes sense that I spent my whole life working in makeup and health. My grandfather: a businessman who loved his work as much as he loved people and who never lost his passion for his job. It makes sense that I started my own company and still have no desire to retire. My grandmother and Aunt Alice: two of the most down-to-earth, comfortable women

I've ever known, who cared more about their family than anything else. It makes sense that my makeup was designed for everyday women, and that I put my family first even as my career grew faster than I could have dreamed.

We all have these threads running through our lives. So many people focus on what they didn't get from their upbringing. I believe understanding and appreciating what you did get is the first step in knowing and accepting yourself. That's not to minimize trauma, or to sell an easy and ultimately unhelpful outlook of mindless positivity. Some things in life are purely negative and must be healed. But in my experience, more often than not, something positive can be found within every negative experience. My strategy is to search for those positives and use them.

At Bobbi Brown Cosmetics, I had this phrase painted on the wall at my office: "So what, now what?" It's a quote from one of my favorite authors, Liz Murray. Murray grew up with drug-addict parents who raised her in squalor and even let her and her sister go hungry as long as they could buy drugs. She ended up being homeless as a teenager but eventually turned her life around and earned a degree from Harvard. In her memoir, *Breaking Night: A Memoir of Forgiveness, Survival, and My Journey from Homelessness to Harvard*, she remembers her parents as loving people who were also terribly flawed. I understand that. My parents, of course, weren't anything like hers. It's the message, rather, that resonates. My parents weren't perfect. So what? Who is? There was darkness and pain in my childhood. Now what? Should I wallow in it? Or should I find a way to move forward?

Of course, no one can be upbeat all the time. But when I'm

down, all I have to do is remember the positive, to think of the ways both of my parents allowed me so many incredible experiences at a young age, showing me all the wonderful, unexpected things that are possible. I feel grateful that I got the best of what they had to offer.

Now what?

PART TWO

KNOW WHO YOU ARE

Ali macGaw

CHAPTER FIVE

REAL FACES

As a child, I wanted to be tall, I wanted to be skinny, I wanted to be athletic, I wanted to be long-limbed, I wanted to be blond. Instead, I was the shortest in my class. I had dark brown hair and dark brown eyes and dark brown eyebrows. I struggled constantly with my weight. No wonder I felt uncomfortable. I was a short Jewish girl in a world of tall Barbies. My friends seemed taller, thinner, and even smarter than me.

As far as I knew, girls who looked like me weren't beautiful, so I tried to change myself. I remember begging my dad to buy me one of those trendy health and wellness books, with a picture of blond bombshell Cheryl Tiegs gracing the cover. The book had all kinds of tips and tricks, exercises, diets, hairdos. None of it worked for me. No matter what I ate, how I styled my hair, how many sit-ups I did, I still looked like myself. It was hard enough competing with my friends in school. How could I compete with Cheryl Tiegs in a bathing suit?

Some girls didn't seem to care about these things, but because of my mother, beauty was a huge part of my consciousness. My mom was glamorous, and I was so not. Yet my mom always thought she could be healthier and thinner. She never met a diet she wouldn't try. And when she tried them, so did I.

These diets would have been comical if they weren't so severe. For instance, the Sexy Pineapple Diet, created by a Danish psychologist, had us eating nothing but pineapple two days a week and eating normally the other days. The creator later admitted he didn't base the diet on science. He just liked pineapple. Imagine me sitting at the kitchen table, stomach rumbling, forking another hunk of pineapple into my mouth, hoping my mother would tire of this diet so I could eat real food. Then there was the HOV diet. That's honey, olive oil, and vinegar in a glass, gulped down. Nope—that didn't work either.

By middle school, I began playing with makeup. I used my mom's hand-me-downs on the way to school. I started on my eyes with powder-blue eye shadow and blue mascara. It was a fun way to pass the time on the school bus, but I also learned some techniques. After one spring break in Florida, I loved the way I looked with a deep tan (the Bain de Soleil years). I figured out how to look even tanner by using my mom's fat bronzing stick from Revlon on my cheeks, forehead, nose, and chin, and a bit under the neck. I made sure to carefully blend it all in. I didn't want anyone to know I was adding to my tan with makeup.

I was starting to see a glimmer of myself looking pretty, but the big *Aha!* moment came when I saw the movie *Love Story* with Ali MacGraw. Ali played Jenny Cavilleri, a working-class college girl who falls in love with a WASP Harvard student named Oliver Barrett IV. Oliver's rich father disapproves of the match and gives his son an ultimatum: choose Jenny or his inheritance. Of course, Oliver chooses Jenny.

Everything about the film moved me, including its famous catchphrase, "Love means never having to say you're sorry." But what moved me most, sitting in that dark theater, was realizing that Ali MacGraw—the beautiful object of all this wonderful romance—looked a little bit like me. She was brunette like me. She had dark hair parted in the middle like me, strong eyebrows like me, and freckles on her nose like me. I saw myself in her. For the first time in my life, I thought, I can be beautiful too.

I noticed something else about Ali in the film. She didn't seem to be wearing any makeup. Of course she was, but she didn't look painted like the other actresses. She just looked like a normal, beautiful person.

In 1970, I was fourteen years old and in the seventh grade—also known as the awkward years. There were a lot of bar mitzvah parties and dress-ups and the start of the new social circle, so I really cared about how I looked. Sometimes I lay face down on an ironing board while my friends drew a warm iron through my wavy hair to straighten it. And sometimes I slept with empty frozen orange juice cans in my hair to do the same. I sunbathed with baby oil and iodine in an empty refrigerator box lined with tinfoil. Yes, I put a lot of effort into my looks. I was also still concerned with my weight and ready to try anything to slim down. By sixteen, I was prescribed diet pills and lost so much weight, my mother had to take me to get all my clothes taken in. She beamed with pride, not realizing I had been going to the pharmacy and getting additional refills, until I ended up fainting on the dressmaker's floor. After watching me faint, my mother made me throw out the pills. Body image was important for her, but even she knew I'd gone too far.

Being thin boosted my self-esteem, and I started to feel attractive. By high school I had a few boyfriends. My first one was an incredibly handsome, model-like athlete who stood six foot four. Even with a broken leg and crutches, he towered over me. We were a sight. I dated my next boyfriend, Larry, for almost five years. He was a year ahead of me in school, very skinny, and looked like John Denver.

Larry was part of my friend group. We'd all meet at the convenience store or Dairy Queen and smoke cigarettes and feel older than we were. Larry and I became a part of each other's family. I was always at his house, or he was at mine.

While I finished my senior year of high school, Larry headed off to college at the University of Wisconsin. Somehow, I managed to graduate a semester early and joined Larry in Oshkosh. Dorm life was super freeing for me, and I optimistically dove in. But Larry and I quickly realized Wisconsin was not the place for us, and together we transferred to the University of Arizona in Tucson, where dozens of our high school buddies were enrolled.

Between the dorm life of four to a room and life in the seventies, it was a nonstop party.

Larry and I also made friends with a long-haired, handsome Jersey boy named Tim. We became the three amigos. We met many days for lunch and watched *Mary Hartman, Mary Hartman.* After our first year, Larry and I returned home to Chicago, and Tim to New Jersey, all of us planning to return the following September.

CHAPTER SIX

MAKEUP UNIVERSITY

When I came home, I realized that I just didn't love being in school. I announced to my mother that I wanted to drop out of college. It was fun but boring, and I couldn't just sit in these auditorium classrooms listening to some professor blab on about something I had no interest in. Mom said I absolutely could not quit. Not an option. I needed to graduate. Then she said the thing that was to change the course of my life. "What would you do if today was your birthday, and you could do anything you wanted?"

I said, "Go to Marshall Field's [a department store in Chicago] and play with makeup."

"That's it," she said. "You should be a makeup artist."

When I said I had no interest in going to beauty school, my mom said there had to be a university where I could study makeup. So I went to the library to search but couldn't find anything. Fortuitously, a friend of my dad's told me Emerson College had a program where you could design your own major. So I gathered my transcripts and planned a visit.

In late August, right before I was supposed to return to Arizona, Tim came into town for a visit, and everything changed. After a year of friendship, we realized we had this intense connection and we were in love. It happened so fast, and it felt so deep. We weren't expecting it, and it took over everything.

My car was packed with Larry's and my things, ready for our cross-country drive back to Arizona. Larry called me the night before we were to leave and said he had something terrible to tell me. He'd realized he was gay and was in love with Tim. I told him I had something worse to tell him: Tim was in love with me, and I was in love with Tim.

Just like that, life changed. Larry's parents came by in the morning and got his things out of my car and just like that I began my next chapter with Tim—a chapter that would last twelve years, from age eighteen to thirty, with more than a few ups and downs and sideways movements. But at that moment, I was just a nice, open-minded kid ready for the next adventure.

When I flew up to Boston to see Emerson, I took one look at this European-style city and was smitten. I had lunch in an outdoor café called the Magic Pan and made my decision to transfer.

At Emerson, I found myself. I created what they called an interdisciplinary major in theatrical makeup, with a minor in photography. I was short some requirements that I'd have to make up, but all the classes were focused on this new BFA major and minor. I was assigned the coolest photography professor as my adviser, and I signed up for public speaking classes and the sole makeup class Emerson offered.

What an eyes-wide-open experience it was. The other students were just like me: creative, excitable, and different. Turns out there is more than one way to learn. It's not that I wasn't smart—I was just a visual learner.

Bring it on.

This curriculum included art history courses, which were a bit boring, but taught me to see the multitude of colors in people's faces. In one of my photography classes, my teacher said, "You see things, but you don't notice them." He would have me take pictures of a pattern: the tiles on a sidewalk, the ripples on the water. These experiences expanded my mind as well as my eyes. I began seeing and noticing. Color was like music to my eyes. For the first time, I was excited to learn.

Another part of my curriculum was to design makeup for theatrical productions. I'd read the plays, visualize the subject, and figure out how to use makeup to make the actors look like the characters. Often the makeup I did was based on the paintings I studied in art history class. I was fascinated to see these characters come to life with the same tools my mother used to get herself ready, the same tools I had used in middle school on the school bus to make up my face for the day. Makeup was becoming my passion.

In film class, we were assigned to write, direct, and edit short films. I went in backward. I thought about what makeup I felt like doing and wrote a script to support that character, often using my good-natured roommate Sarah as the star. For one film, I made up Sarah as an old, sad woman who was homebound and ate dog food out of a can. I covered her face in pasty white makeup and used a dark pencil to create wrinkles. Her white hair was made with a mop and bedsheets. Thankfully, it was shot in black and white, so you couldn't see how unprofessional it was. I had her looking so sad. She tried not to giggle as she fell out the window to end the movie.

Soon I started making up everyone in the dorm. I made them look like clowns, or boxers with bruises on their faces. I did the same things to my brother and stepbrothers when I was home from college. My dad once fell asleep on a hammock and woke up with a makeover. In these moments, I realized, this is who I am supposed to be.

The next three years passed quickly. I graduated with a BFA in theatrical makeup and a minor in photography. Worried about paying my rent, I stayed in Boston and got a job as a waitress after lying about my experience. I learned two important things: how hard it is to be a waitress, and how to calculate 20 percent of any number, as I anticipated my tips.

My first makeup gig in Boston came quickly: a docudrama about teenage alcoholism, directed by a Boston filmmaker. I had to put a fake bruise on the actor's eye, only this time I had to remember exactly how I did it so I could re-create it in the future. Movies are shot out of sequence, which meant I had to re-create the bruise on one day, then do something completely different the next day, then put the bruise back in exactly the same place and in exactly the same way the day after that. It was boring and tedious. I knew this was not going to be my path.

I thought maybe I'd try television instead, and my stepfather recommended I contact his cousin, a successful and well-known television writer and producer in Los Angeles who wrote for Sid Caesar's *Caesar's Hour* with Mel Brooks and Carl Reiner, as well as episodes of *M*A*S*H* and *The Dick Van Dyke Show*. I wrote to him explaining my background and what I hoped to do. I was looking for a start. Months later, I received a response: he had marked up my letter like an English teacher, correcting all the grammar, and said, "Work on your grammar and delivery before you write anyone another letter."

It was a blow, but his response made me pause. And once I let the rejection go, I was inspired to find another career path. For the next year, I stayed in Boston working as a waitress and trying to get makeup gigs, but there was already one makeup artist there who seemed to have the local market cornered. I accepted that I wouldn't find the kind of work I wanted in Boston. So I decided to move to New York City.

PART THREE

FIGURE IT OUT

CHAPTER SEVEN

GO SEE

New York City in 1980 was a wild place. A garbage strike left the streets covered in trash; two epidemics—crack and AIDS—had begun their deadly work; the Guardian Angels patrolled the subways in a brave but vain attempt to stop rampant muggings; and John Lennon was shot and killed outside his apartment building.

In awe of the city, I hardly noticed. I moved into a ground-floor apartment with Tim on West Fourth Street and walked around the Village in big puffy socks, short shorts, permed hair, and hoop earrings, looking like an extra from *Flashdance*. I was a suburban

Midwestern kid mesmerized by the city's endless energy and possibilities.

For my college graduation present, my father gifted me rent for a year while I established myself. My early days in New York I spent filling my date book, making friends with the gay hairdressers I met at makeup tests, and taking exercise classes. Everyone seemed larger than life, including a girl in my exercise class who was an incredible dancer. She always stood in the back row, but I couldn't take my eyes off her. One day she didn't come back. I learned she was shooting a movie. Her name was Madonna.

Having no idea how to break into makeup, I decided to return to waitressing. In one day of interviewing, I got four rejections. This experience was much too difficult for a job I didn't want to do anyway. *If I'm going to get rejected*, I thought, *it might as well be for something I care about.* From that point on, I poured all my effort into building a career in makeup.

I put an ad in *The Village Voice*: "Makeup artist available to give lessons." I got one call—a guy from Connecticut, who wore Gucci loafers and had a giant Louis Vuitton bag full of women's clothes. "I'm an actor and am doing a role," he lied. "I'd love to learn how to do makeup as a woman." He went through several changes of skimpy lingerie, asking me to change the makeup for each outfit. I never put an ad in the paper again.

Next I opened up the Yellow Pages, found "makeup," and saw that there was a makeup union. I didn't know a union from a dance troupe, but I called and made an appointment in the Midtown Manhattan office. There I met the head of the union.

"I'm here to sign up for the union," I said.

He chuckled. "That's not how it works," he said.

"Tell me how it works, then," I said, thinking he'd have me fill out some paperwork and I'd get in.

"If you're not bloodline and don't know anyone, it takes years." he said.

"Years?"

"Six, seven years, kid."

I certainly wasn't bloodline. I didn't know anyone, had no recommendations, and barely even had a portfolio. For some reason, though, he liked me. He promised to throw me temporary work as an apprentice while I did my time to get in the union. Through him, I began to receive occasional offers for low-level makeup gigs. I started working on the local news, touching up the newscasters. I remember one particular newscaster who had a terrible attitude and a big booger in his nose. I considered letting him go on the air like that, but ultimately decided doing a good job was more important than petty revenge. I also worked on *Saturday Night Live* a few times as a freelancer, and even got to do makeup for Julia Louis-Dreyfus on the show. What a thrill it was to be a part of this hip, culture-defining show I used to watch in my living room with my high school friends.

These temporary gigs didn't pay much, though, and I was struggling to make ends meet. I called my dad and said, "I need help learning to budget." He gave me a piece of life-changing advice: "I'm not going to teach you how to budget. Figure out how you are going to make more money." This was exactly what I needed to hear.

Before leaving Boston, I had read an article in *Mademoiselle* magazine about a freelance makeup artist named Bonnie Maller who did all the makeup for fashion shows, from Calvin Klein to Ralph Lauren, and magazines, from *Vogue* to *Glamour*, as well as ad campaigns. I wrote her a letter offering free assistance but never heard back. When I moved to New York, I called her again. She never called me back, but her answering machine said if it was a call about work, to contact her agent, Bryan Bantry. So I did.

Bryan's office was on Fifty-Fifth Street. I brought my portfolio, filled with mostly things I had done in college and whatever I could scrape together of my freelance work. I arrived at the office, a bundle of nerves, took a breath, and composed myself. Walking into a big New York building with important New York people, I felt like I had hit the big time. Bryan represented several of the top photographers, hairstylists, and makeup artists in the business. I didn't know if I'd have five minutes or an hour with him, but I wanted to nail it.

The office was so cool. Framed magazine covers lined the walls, along with calendars tracking all the different artists, models, and photographers he represented. He was really busy. He had little time to sit and chat. He looked at my portfolio and got right to the point. "You need tear sheets." Tear sheets are examples of your work that you'd sometimes literally tear out of a magazine. I knew I needed them. No kidding, I thought. How am I going to get them when I can't get magazine work? Though he didn't offer to represent me, Bryan did say he'd help me and he'd call the next time he needed to hire a makeup assistant for a shoot.

I left that meeting feeling optimistic. I believed Bryan would come through for me, and I made it a habit to keep in touch with him, but I didn't just wait for his call. As my first year in New York wound down, and with it my promised rent money, I developed a routine. On Mondays, I'd buy the fashion magazines, look at the mastheads, and identify the photographers, booking agents, and editors and cold-call them. "Hi, I'm Bobbi Brown, I'm a freelance makeup artist, and I'd like to show you my book." Then I'd make an appointment with anyone who would see me—appointments are known as "go-sees" in the business. You literally go see someone with your portfolio and hope they hire you.

I also went to the modeling agencies and met with the model bookers there. The agents always needed makeup artists for their newest models, who did photo shoots known as makeup tests for their portfolios. On these shoots, everyone worked for free in exchange for photos for our portfolios. We were all newbies, honing our craft and getting a nice photo to put in our book, and building a network. Sometimes the photographer or stylist would need a makeup artist on a small paid gig, and I'd get a call. It was a great way to learn, and it sure beat waiting tables.

My job was to push myself, to do what I needed to find work. I knew there were dozens of people trying to see these photographers, bookers, and editors. I had to be relentless—and nice—to make sure I was the one invited in, and back in. After each gig, I stayed in touch with my contacts, and I made sure to keep improving my work so that when I called and said, "Hi, this is Bobbi Brown again," I had something new to show them.

One day Bryan Bantry called me in to work as an assistant to

Mariella Smith Masters, who had a big advertising job for a high-end fashion company shooting a fragrance ad. My job was to slather a male model with Vaseline and then apply glitter makeup to his naked body . . . that was fun.

I soon learned that fashion is a small world. Frequently, the same people would rehire me because I arrived on time with a smile, and I was happy to do any menial job. On set, I kept an eye out for anything I could do to help, even if it was just getting someone water or holding a reflector. I was obsessed with doing a good job.

Slowly, these small, random jobs turned into a client list. I was becoming a regular. Around this time, I was hired to assist makeup artist Linda Mason at Fashion Week. I had taken a class Linda taught in her apartment a few months earlier, and now I had a chance to work with her. Linda was, and still is, one of the world's most creative makeup artists. She was famous for using crazy, bold, neon slashes of color on a model's face. She taught me how to use a freer and bolder hand and also how to let loose and throw makeup on the face (literally take a brush and splatter it on the face, like an abstract artist). Later in my career, I would do my own version of Linda's makeup for magazine shoots.

Fashion Week is a crucial event in the industry. It sets the trends for the season, but it's also like an art show that pushes the boundaries of clothing and makeup. Assisting a bigger artist was a great way to get my name out there and it was exhilarating to be a part of these shows.

I carried Linda's makeup bags, organized them, and got her tools ready as she worked on the models. Because I was a newcomer, I often just stood there and watched as Linda or her assistants with more experience than me did their work. But if there were lots of models at once, I'd jump in and do the makeup and wait for her to check it. It either looked okay or they'd fix it, and that's how I learned. Then I'd do touch-ups, clean up after the show ended, and head home exhausted from spending twelve hours on my feet. At home, I'd replay the day in my head and try to see what I could have done better. This was important to me. I always wanted to improve and be called back. I still do.

One Fashion Week gig was for WilliWear by Willi Smith, an influential African American designer. He always had these gorgeous Black and mixed-race models. It was far from the norm in fashion at the time, and that excited me. In fact, everything about that show excited me. I had never worked on such a large stage before. The pace was tremendous and so were the stakes. Millions of people would see the photographs of these models, and an entire clothing line was being launched on their backs. It was high intensity and tons of fun. On that shoot, I met an assistant stylist named Cathy who later would hire me to be the head artist on the shows when she was lead stylist. She would also eventually introduce me to the love of my life.

I think it was my commitment to improving, along with being an easygoing and positive person, that made people want to hire me. The phone began to ring more and more, and I slowly left the entry-level gigs behind. It took a couple of years, but I began to find my people, to work my way up the ranks, and most important, to make a living. I no longer relied on Bryan Bantry or the union representative to toss me a few bones. I never did make it into that union, but by my mid-twenties, I finally became a working makeup artist.

COSMOPOLITAN

September 1985 • 8

If porn's
free
why is
erotica
under
wraps?

**The bucks
start here**
Our report
means
business!

Chic Labour
Kinnock & Co
have designs
on you

- Make a
man talk
- Win a
£5000 holiday
- Spot the
Hollywood brats
- Mange-tout
in Paris

**Jerry Ha
an
othe
Scarle
wome**

Wh
D H Lawreno
is love
fallen ang

Is fashic
goir
off the rail

**Mad abou
book**
Me
Angela Carto
Margaret Drabb
D M Thoma
Fay Weldo
at Cosmo
Book Da

CHAPTER EIGHT

GLITZ AND GLAMOUR

The main goal of makeup back then (in the 1980s) was to cover, to change, to distort. Foundation was pink (or gray for women of color). The look was artificial. Eye makeup was purple, yellow, blue. There was a lot of painting and contouring of eyes, cheeks, and lips. I never quite understood that. As much as I revered the great makeup I saw in magazines, I could never apply makeup like that. I always wanted people to look like themselves, only a little healthier. I felt best when, after applying makeup to a model, it looked like they weren't wearing makeup at all.

Around that time I showed a well-known makeup artist my makeup on the cover model of an Italian magazine and asked his advice. He told me it was too natural, and if I wanted to be a makeup artist working in high fashion, I had to do it in the style that was happening then. I couldn't and I didn't. I kept on trying to be my best, and to get hired to do what I did: a more natural makeup technique.

I kept learning on the job, which soon included catalog work for major department stores like Lord & Taylor, Saks Fifth Avenue, and Macy's. These were always pleasant shoots. There was no pressure to redefine haute couture. We were nice, normal people doing a job for a nice, normal store so they could advertise their clothes. This gave me a chance to work with many different models and photographers, to enhance my artistic eye, and to refine my skill with color. Even better, the shoots lasted a week or more, which felt like a steady job.

Normally, I packed a massive makeup kit the night before the shoot (I still have back problems from those bags), then spent all day on set playing with color, only to lug it all back home each night, open the bag, throw everything on the floor, and reorganize it all for the next shoot.

It served a purpose. Wanting to streamline, I'd make piles of every eye shadow, every lipstick, every blush, then sort them by color and look at them critically until I finally figured out: I don't need seventeen taupes. I need one or two. I liked the taupes that weren't orange, but I didn't want them to be gray. The next day, I'd show up on set with my bag fifteen taupes lighter. I also made a fun kit full of crazy colors, but I only brought that to editorial work with a more experimental photographer, and that bag went through the most drastic cuts. This process of paring, editing, and optimizing took years—and it has never really stopped. All my practical knowledge began to develop here.

Working for catalogs gave me great stability, but I knew the real work for any serious makeup artist came from the fashion magazines. The top, the peak, the zenith was *Vogue*. It was the only American high-fashion magazine, and it was always the most important. It hired the best of the best, the top photographers and the top hair and makeup artists. Next came the lower-tier magazines like *Glamour*, *Mademoiselle*, *Marie Claire*, and *Elle*, which were aimed at the new working girl. These were important magazines, but not high fashion. A rung below these were what we called women's magazines or "shelter" magazines: *Redbook*, *First for Women*, *Good Housekeeping*. Those reached the masses, and I would soon learn that when you have your own brand, they are invaluable sources. After that, you had the arty, avant-garde magazines like *Interview* and *i-D*.

I ate these magazines for breakfast, lunch, and dinner. I studied them deeply, not just to see the names on the masthead, but also to look at the art, the lighting, the makeup. I knew more about the craft now, and I noticed more, just like I did in my college photography classes. When I saw a picture that spoke to me, I'd try to figure out how they'd created the effect. Then, when I was on set, I'd use those pictures for inspiration, just like I used to do with classic paintings in college.

I got one of my first big breaks in fashion magazines on a cover shoot for British *Cosmopolitan* magazine with Jerry Hall. I had never felt so nervous. She was on every magazine cover, a supermodel superstar married to Mick Jagger, and I was an up-and-comer who was thrilled just to be on set. After I finished doing her makeup and handed her a mirror, she said, "Thank you, it's lovely. Do you mind if I touch it up?" I said, "Of course not." She proceeded to completely change most of what I had done. She contoured every inch of her face, from her eyes to her nose to her jawbone to her cheeks. I didn't feel bad, maybe because she was so nice about it. Instead, I took it as a learning opportunity.

I was in awe of Jerry. I was also bad at the eighties style of makeup expected of me. I couldn't overline, paint, and contour like everyone else. Sometimes I felt inferior. But instead of quitting, I kept working on my craft and trying to improve my skills. For instance, I was often asked to take a dark eye shadow and do a smoky blended eye, but I couldn't get it right. So I figured out a way to layer the color, to start with something light, add a medium tone, and go deeper until I achieved the same effect. I didn't know it, but the techniques I was teaching myself became the reason people hired me instead of someone else, and they ended up turning into a point of difference for my first brand when I began to teach women how to be their own makeup artist.

There were many other times when I had to find the courage to admit I had made a mistake and say, "Yikes! You have to wash your face so I can start over." I remember an early location shoot in a funky Hampton hotel with the model Kim Alexis. We needed to get her ready to shoot by sunrise, so she had to come to my hotel room while it was still dark outside. The only light was a standing lamp, where I set up my kit and got to work. By the time I finished, the sun was rising. In the light of day, I realized the makeup I had done was horrible. We were running late, but when the editor came in,

I said, "I have to do this over again." Somehow, I was able to slap it on in time, and it looked way better now that I could see what I was doing. Boy, did I learn the importance of good lighting then.

There were many makeup artists who inspired me. I took little bits from each one. Top artist Alberto Fava had a way with silver, and used it just so, so it highlighted the face. Way Bandy, who did most of the *Cosmopolitan* covers, was an incredible painter of the face and beloved by many. He was also the creator of a Calvin Klein cosmetics line that was so ahead of its time, no one bought it. By the time I found it, it was half-price at Bloomingdale's. Natural makeup wasn't part of the beauty landscape yet, and people said, "What are all these dull browns?" But I loved them, and they inspired me for years, especially when I began creating my own line. I can still see them clear as day in my head.

I also learned an enormous amount from the photographer Bruce Weber. One day, I got a call from Bryan Bantry, saying, "Bruce has a shoot for Italian *Vogue*, and Bonnie Maller can't do it. Can you fill in?" The only thing I thought, other than *Yes, of course!* was *Why would anyone cancel on Bruce Weber?!* But Bonnie was ahead of me in her career. She had reached the point all artists dream of, where you don't have to take any job that comes your way. She probably had a better offer with more money for another shoot. This left the incredibly cool yet low-paying job at Italian *Vogue* to someone like me. I'd eventually learn the challenges of the makeup world, and how hard these choices were to make. You could work your way up to the top—the best photographers, models, editors, magazines— and they'd hire you over and over again, until you weren't available, and then someone else would take your place, and you might never get another call from them. Someone like Bonnie, though, was so seasoned that she'd find work no matter what. I aspired to reach that level.

I spent hours the night before the shoot organizing my makeup bag and agonizing over what to wear, desperately wanting to make a good first impression. I suffered from the beginner's fear of wondering if I was good enough, cool enough to work with these people, or if they'd see through me and never hire me again. The next morning, I got to the studio, which was a warehouse in downtown Manhattan, knocked on the door, and was greeted by a guy with a bushy beard, a giant smile, and a bandanna on his head. Bruce.

"Hi, Bobbi," he said. "It's so nice to meet you. I've been waiting a long time to work with you."

I still don't know if he'd actually heard of me or was just being nice, but I was dumbfounded. He was waiting to work with me? That kindness meant everything. I would take it with me throughout my career, and when I became the person young artists were nervous wrecks to work with, I always tried to make them feel as welcome as Bruce had made me feel.

Despite Bruce's welcome, I still had butterflies in my stomach, as I always did when walking onto a new set. We were shooting two young models/actors named Matt Dillon and Talisa Soto. I got down to work, doing what I thought was the right thing. Bruce took one look at Talisa and said, "Too much makeup, honey. Please take it down."

I started over, trying to give him the more natural look he wanted, which fit my natural inclination anyway. Then I watched how he worked. He'd get behind the camera and tell Talisa: "Bite your lip.

Pinch your cheek." I saw all these colors come out that I had never noticed before. That's when I realized everyone has a unique combination of colors blended naturally into their skin. It's subtle, and you need to really pay attention to see it, but it's there. The colors differ from person to person, but also from one part of the face to another. The eyelids aren't the same as the cheeks. Everyone's lips are a different color.

Learning to see the colors was the first step in learning to enhance them with makeup. I just had to blend the right colors to match the different areas of the face. The more I worked with Bruce, who kept hiring me, the more I noticed that when I complemented these natural colors in the skin, the models looked better. This was another Ali McGraw moment. I realized that in this world of makeup artists who acted like avant-garde painters, there was space for someone like me who just wanted women to look naturally beautiful.

CHAPTER NINE

CLIMB THE LADDER

By the mid-eighties, my phone rarely stopped ringing. I could pay my rent and support myself doing what I loved. More important, I was finding my people in the fashion world. I signed with an agent named Dan Brennan. I had a thick portfolio with good tear sheets, which made it easy for him to get me jobs, and when he did, it was no longer as an assistant. Now I was the lead makeup artist.

As the lead artist, I had a seat at the big table. During magazine shoots, I was part of the early conversation with the editor, the stylist, and the photographer. They still told me what they wanted me to do, but now I had the power to say, "Yeah, that's good, but have you thought of this?" I loved those discussions.

The days on a magazine shoot were long. I'd arrive early in the morning and ask: "What do you want to accomplish? How do we do it? What's the lighting? Is the shoot inside or outside? Do you want makeup or hair done first?" The answers to these questions gave me the information I needed to start creating my plan, but nothing really mattered until the models arrived. Some were punctual; others floated in hours after the call time without so much as an apology. Then we'd sit over coffee and a beautiful breakfast. All the while I'd be studying the girls, trying to catch them in certain ways to see the shape of their faces, how the light hit them, what colors were in their skin, and what makeup colors might work to complement that.

Then I got to work. Usually, I prepared the skin first with moisturizer and eye cream. The toughest area was under the eyes, because I didn't want the models to look tired, but if I used too much makeup it looked like they had cake under their eyes, and the concealer colors were so white. I'd let the moisturizer and eye cream settle, apply concealer, foundation, powder, and blush, then do the eyes. I learned to do the lips last because there were usually several hours before the shoot and in that time the model would probably eat or smoke—or, since it was the 1980s, snort cocaine.

Sometimes the photographers loved what I had done, sometimes they didn't. Maybe the stylist would vent her rage on me. I eventually got used to those nerve-racking moments waiting to see if they liked my makeup or not. But I was more worried about not being booked again, which happened more than once. When it did, my head immediately returned to the place of "I wasn't good enough, I wasn't cool enough." It was like being in high school again, feeling I wasn't smart enough, pretty enough, tall enough. I think all artists go through this process. No matter how confident or successful you become, you still have to wrestle the voices of doubt.

Leading a fashion show was similar to leading a magazine shoot, except that I got to hire and direct my own team. Mostly I hired people I had met during my work as an assistant, people I liked and vibed with. For Adrienne Vittadini's show, I'd hire four or five makeup assistants, plus a personal assistant for me alone. Often my personal assistant had little-to-no makeup experience—I just liked them and thought they had a spark. They'd carry my makeup bag and arrange it the way I liked it: skincare first, then concealers, foundations, powders, blushes, shadows, brushes in a cup, and a little area for my what-ifs like Q-tips, cleaning solution, powder puffs. When I was the lead makeup artist, one thing was constant: the ultimate responsibility was mine. I basked in the praise if the models looked good, and I withered under the criticism if they didn't.

When work got slow, as often happens in the industry, I'd call my agent three, four, or five times a day: "What's going on? Is anyone calling? Are other people working?" It took a long time and a lot of experience to learn that's just how the business goes. It's feast or famine. Sometimes I had more work than I could handle; sometimes the phone wouldn't ring for two weeks. It wasn't necessarily because of anything I did or didn't do or because I wore the wrong outfit. It's easy to look back on it now and see that. It was much harder in the moment.

As I began to receive bigger jobs and expand my posse of photographers, models, and editors, my work started to become more glamorous, exotic, and exciting. At the start of each year, the shoots would take me to Jamaica, Anguilla, the Bahamas. It was usually the same setup: we'd stay in some funky hotel and wake up before the restaurant opened to catch the light at sunrise. We wouldn't eat breakfast until lunchtime. In the heat of the afternoon, we'd have lavish, boozy lunches, return to our rooms to nap, then wake up to catch the light at sunset. After a late dinner of fried grouper, fried grouper, or fried grouper, we'd collapse to do it again the next day, and the next day, and the next one. It was exhausting. By the end of four or five days, you'd be best friends with everybody, you'd have had your little flings on a romantic island together with nothing else to do—and then all of a sudden you'd have to say goodbye to this new family and go home to the snow, gray skies, and darkness in the afternoon, feeling exhausted and worn out from it all.

On these shoots, I spent a lot of time with European photographers and models. I was a sponge, studying how they buttoned their sleeves and tucked in their shirts, what kind of shoes they wore. I remember the amazing hairstylist Didier Malige wore the most beautiful loafers I've ever seen, and I asked him where he got them. He said in his thick Parisian accent, "Zey make zem for me." Of course they did. I didn't want to seem stupid with all these chic, hip people. Somehow I had become part of this world, but I never really felt I truly belonged to it. I wasn't an artist; I was hired for the simple, natural look, not high fashion. I couldn't compete with these uber-successful artists like Kevyn Aucoin and Way Bandy and I didn't want to. I always jumped at the chance to work on these kinds of shoots, but I wanted to be the best at my kind of makeup. The more jobs I worked on, the more people I met who appreciated that about me.

It took courage to go my own way. Once, on a job for an Italian magazine, I experimented on set using a big fat bronzer and blending it all over the model's face. She looked so beautiful. I put the bronzer on her lips and eyes, too, to get a tan monochromatic look. No one did that back then. It seemed too simple. There were no big splashes of color, no dark smoky eyes, no candy-apple lips. There was just a beautiful woman with beautiful skin who looked beautiful herself. The photograph was used on the magazine's cover. Proud of my work, I showed it to a well-known makeup artist I knew. "If you can't do what people want, you're never going to work," he said. This guy was doing *Vogue* covers. I felt rejected. But I didn't hold on to it for very long, and I didn't take his advice. At twenty-seven years old, I had begun to define myself and my vision.

The more I succeeded, the harder I pushed myself to improve. I was lucky to book a shoot with the Chinese-Jamaican photographer Walter Chin (and luckier to stay in his posse for many years). During the shoot, he said, "Bobbi, mon, come here and look at the makeup from yesterday." He handed me a loupe, which is like a little magnifying glass, and I saw that the face and body didn't match. "When you do the models today," Walter said, "please make up their body too."

This is dumb, I thought. I was tired of going to Bergdorf Goodman and buying expensive makeup to slather all over a model's body, so I decided to reverse the process, matching the color of the foundation to the natural colors of the model's body. Unfortunately,

I couldn't find foundations that matched real body or skin tones in the department stores. Now what?

I started shopping at theatrical makeup stores as I did in college, where the makeup was cheaper and I could mix it until it was exactly the shade I wanted. For lighter-skinned models, I found that yellow tones in foundation worked better than standard foundations because when they had a lot of red and pink in them, it looked fake. For darker skin, I'd add a touch of orange, red, or blue and create more rich brown tones.

By alternating foundations and experimenting with theatrical makeup, I realized I had found a way to improve not just the cosmetic photo shoots but also the makeup itself, while making my work easier. I began to believe there was something wrong with the whole industry. Makeup, even at the big brands like Chanel and Estée Lauder, was created by marketing and product-development people. I wondered, why don't actual makeup artists have a say in the creation of the product?

I also developed other techniques to improve my work. Often during a shoot, something would go wrong with the makeup that was too minor to notice until we saw the film the next day. So I would bring a pair of opera binoculars and sit in the back of the studio peering through the binoculars, obsessing over every detail. Does she need more blush? Powder between her brows? Blending under the eyes? Are the lashes stuck together? In this way, I could identify the mistakes while we were shooting, saving us time and money.

As more magazines featured my makeup, they also began to include me in the story. This elevated my profile. I was someone who could work behind the camera making up the models to achieve someone else's vision, and also appear in front of it, in a photo doing the models' makeup. Beneath a picture of the makeup, you might read something like, "Bobbi Brown says choose the color of your blush by the color of your cheeks when you exercise." Gradually it was more than just my work that had currency. My name did too.

CHAPTER TEN

ONE DOOR CLOSES . . .

As I was working my way up in the fashion world, my boyfriend Tim was doing the same in photography. We moved to a loft apartment on Thirty-Seventh Street that doubled as Tim's photo studio, where he began the work that would eventually make him a celebrated portrait photographer. The problem was, Tim loved the rock 'n' roll lifestyle, and our breakups usually resulted from the fact that he didn't want to get married or have kids and end up in the suburbs. During the twelve years we were together, we broke up many times. But Tim always returned, and I always took him back. I accepted more than I should have. I was young, naive, and in love.

I didn't know the final breakup with Tim was final at first. I'll never forget when he told me, "Go find that Jewish man you're looking for."

I moved out and sublet an apartment in Greenwich Village from the model Stella Hall, who had recently been broken up with by John McEnroe. She'd painted the entire apartment pink, because she found the color healing.

Devastated, I cried all day in my pink apartment. I called my friend Cathy, whom I had met during my first Fashion Week, and poured out my troubles. We made plans to have dinner together. "Where do you want to go?" she asked. I mentioned three restaurants I liked: Raoul's, Indochine, and Florent. She didn't want to go to any of these. "I'll just meet you at your apartment, and we'll decide," she said. "By the way," she added, "I'd like to bring my friend Steven. Do you mind if he comes?"

Unbeknownst to me, Cathy had been telling Steven about me for years. "Bobbi is so fabulous. Bobbi and her boyfriend are going to this cool party. Bobbi's on a shoot in the Caribbean." According to Steven, when he finally met me, he felt like he was meeting a celebrity.

I didn't look my best after crying all day, wearing no makeup, with my hair in a ponytail, but I couldn't have been more myself. Standing in my apartment, Cathy asked Steven where he wanted to eat, and he said, "How about Raoul's? Or maybe Indochine? Or Florent?"

Fate or coincidence?

We went to Raoul's, a charming little French bistro in SoHo where the conversation eventually came around to Tim.

"We're on a break," I sighed, "but we'll probably get back together."

"You're not getting back together," Steven said.

I guess he knew something I didn't. After dinner, Steven and I shared a cab back to my place. We stood outside my apartment talking for hours. I went upstairs, climbed in bed, stared at the ceiling the entire night, and called my dad in the morning.

"I just met the man I'm going to marry," I said.

"What's his name?" Dad asked.

"Steven."

"What does he do?"

"I don't know"

"Is he Jewish?"

"I don't know."

"What's his last name?"

"I don't know."

On our second date, I learned Steven was Jewish, had a graduate degree from Harvard, and owned his own real estate development company, but his last name was Plofker. Oh, well. It was a total out-of-body experience. There was just this electric connection, emotional and deep. I know it doesn't happen for everyone. I got lucky. Thirty-seven years later, we have never left each other's side.

Of course, Tim came back and said, "I made a mistake. I do

want to get married. I want kids." For a nanosecond I thought, Am I throwing away this twelve-year relationship for a guy I just met? But Steven was so solid, so strong, and had piercing blue eyes. It felt like something major was happening. The nanosecond passed.

In the fall of 1987, a few weeks after I met Steven, I was hired for an Adrienne Vittadini shoot in Mexico. I had worked with Adrienne and her crew many times, so they were all privy to my grief with Tim. This time, though, they could tell something had changed. I couldn't stop talking about this new guy. One day after a shoot, I returned to find the housekeeper in my hotel room. She said, "Amor, amor," and gestured to the window. Steven was standing on my veranda. He had hopped on a few planes and found me.

Just before Christmas, Steven and I took a trip to Santa Fe. He does most things spontaneously, so all the hotels were booked, but he found an adobe house through the reservationist at one of the hotels he called. Those days felt as magical as the snow-covered mesa outside, but in the middle of this intense, romantic time, I still felt the angst of everything that had happened with Tim. That's when Steven said, "You might have to get back together with Tim one more time to see if you really want to be with me." The very idea sounded so ridiculous. That's when I knew without any doubt Steven was the one.

Back in New York a few months later, my lease at the pink apartment ended. Steven told me not to sign another lease, which in New York is like saying, "Move in with me." But I had lived with Tim for so long and I didn't want to do it again. "I'm not living with anyone until I get engaged," I told Steven. A few weeks later, he took me ice skating in Central Park, got down on one knee, and proposed. I was stunned. We'd been dating only three months, but I think we both knew.

On September 10, 1988—nine months after our first date—I married Steven at the Woolverton Inn near New Hope, Pennsylvania. The wedding was dreamy. The famous hairdresser Oribe did my hair. Three hundred people came to celebrate our union, many on buses from New York City. A funny female rabbi from the University of Pennsylvania did the ceremony, and a band of Broadway musicians played until the wee hours of the morning. Then we took a three-week honeymoon, the first part of which I planned at the Rancho La Puerta spa on the California–Mexico border.

I had started pitching story ideas to magazines. It was a good way to get work without having to wait for work to come to me. I always saw possibilities. I guess that's part of being an entrepreneur, but it's also the Papa Sam in me. I don't remember how I came up with the idea, or why Steven agreed to it, but I pitched a story on our honeymoon to *New Body* magazine. It was all around the concept of wellness. While Steven and I honeymooned together, they took pictures of us running, hiking, and enjoying the spa.

Steven planned the rest of the honeymoon as a surprise. "Pack for anything," he said. After Rancho La Puerta, we flew to Canada and visited Banff, Jasper, and Lake Louise. Then we rented a car and drove around to all these Montana dude ranches while I wrote the thank-you notes for our wedding gifts.

It was the furthest thing from New York City imaginable, which was the direction my life was heading. The day we returned from our honeymoon, we closed on a house in the town of Montclair, New Jersey. It required a long renovation before we could leave the city and move in. It all happened so fast, and I certainly didn't expect any of it. I was living a cool New York life, working on these hip fashion shoots, making a name for myself as a makeup artist. All of a sudden my chic world didn't seem quite as interesting as Steven and what we might create together.

VOGUE

SEPTEMBER $

THE
BIGGEST
FASHION
ISSUE!

FALL
THE
MOST
EXCITING
LOOKS

CHAPTER ELEVEN

COVER GIRL 1989

A decade had passed since I'd arrived in New York City with a dream, a good work ethic, and not much else. I'd figured out how to talk my way into getting people to meet with me, to hustle odd jobs, to make myself useful even when I didn't know what I was doing, and to keep my eyes open for the opportunities. Whether working as a makeup assistant for the local news, *Saturday Night Live*, or Fashion Week, or as the lead artist for Macy's, Saks, or *Glamour*, I approached every job with the same attitude: work hard and get better. I didn't believe my success was guaranteed. I had achieved a lot. I was able to travel the world with fabulous models and photographers. I had established myself in the industry. Most important, I had remained true to myself and my vision. But there was one thing I still hadn't achieved: my makeup hadn't graced the cover of *Vogue*.

Before my wedding, Andrea Q. Robinson, the beauty editor at *Vogue*, had hired me to do a shoot on the different looks for the season. The photographer was the respected and talented Wayne Maser. The model, Tatjana Patitz, was an unusual beauty. She had very deep-set, piercing blue eyes. I wanted to do something different with her makeup, something as unique as her face. I tried a few unusual things, like putting foundation on her lips and blotting them down with blush or using lipstick on her cheeks to give a little sheen. Andrea was there, often encouraging me to go even further with my vision. I loved working with her.

The pictures came out great. But I had learned that no matter how good I thought the pictures were, I never knew if they would be used. The editor in chief might throw the pictures in the garbage, chop them up, or shrink them down. Or I might get a full-page bleed. So when the 1989 edition of *Vogue* hit the stands, I was surprised to find a six-page spread inside, with just the model's face on every page, and beneath it the line: "Makeup by Bobbi Brown."

When I look back at these photographs and photo shoots, I see they don't look that different from the kind of makeup I'm doing today. It was clean and pretty, and that's what I was becoming known for. My girls could finish the shoot, put on their jeans, and walk out the door without even washing their face. I was proud of that.

Not long after that *Vogue* shoot, Andrea went to work at Revlon.

She asked me to be her creative director, but I turned her down. I didn't want to be part of a corporation, and I couldn't imagine working in an office.

Still, I appreciated Andrea's help getting me further into *Vogue*, and it didn't take long until I was hired for 1989's September issue.

September was the most important and largest edition of the year, with the most advertising pages. This made the work extra important. We went to the Hamptons with Patrick Demarchelier to shoot the supermodel Naomi Campbell. I had a vision of Naomi's makeup: simple, elegant, with a blackberry stain on her lips. She was known at the time for taking a dark lip liner, softening the edges, and putting a light color on the inside of her lip. That was her look, not mine. Naomi likely hated the makeup I did that day, but I didn't ask what she thought of it, and there were no mirrors on the beach, so I went with my vision.

A few months later, I was on another shoot somewhere in New York City, sitting in the back of a van, when Steven called me. "I have a surprise," he said. He pulled up a few minutes later and entered the van with the September 1989 edition of *Vogue* in his hands. There, on the cover, her blackberry lips parted in a dazzling smile, was Naomi Campbell.

"You made the cover," he said.

Ecstasy, joy, bliss, jubilation. I felt them all. Tunnel vision, time, and perseverance had led me to the epicenter of the fashion world. My dream came true. *Great,* I thought. *What's next?*

PART FOUR

WHAT IF/ WHY NOT

CHAPTER TWELVE

THE BURBS

Steven and I closed on our first house the day we returned from our honeymoon, but the move to Montclair happened gradually. While we renovated the house, I stayed in the city and worked. Steven drove back and forth to check on the progress daily. I'd see it on the weekends. Then my life seemed to change overnight. When the house was ready, I left New York, the place where I had defined myself as a working adult, and moved to the suburbs.

It took me a little while to recalibrate. When we first moved, Steven and I went to dinner in the middle of a suburban strip mall off a highway. I looked at Steven like, *What the hell did we just do?* Slowly, we found our place and our crowd. As much as I loved New York, Montclair fit us better. I loved the town, the grass, the backyard, the community. Everything in Manhattan was hard, from the subways to the traffic to the noise to the grit and grime. Often getting from my apartment to work was a difficult journey. In Montclair, everything was easy. I chose normalcy over fabulosity. At the end of each workday, I'd go through the Lincoln Tunnel and breathe a sigh of relief. Though we kept an apartment in the city, we almost never used it. By our first wedding anniversary, I was pregnant.

As my life changed, so did my work. The constant traveling had begun to wear on me. Yes, I loved traveling around the world and experiencing beautiful, exotic places and people. But I was getting tired of waking up at four-thirty in the morning, and eating whatever food was available. I felt tired and bloated much of the time. I was afraid of flying, and I missed my bed and my routine. I'm still the same way today, and I was the same as a kid. My mother had to pick me up from sleepovers and take me home to my own bed. I started declining Caribbean trips and fancy magazine shoots in order to make it home for dinner. I had different priorities. I put my family first.

The Caribbean work went to other people who would jump on a plane and stay on a set until sunrise if necessary. I'd open the magazines to see what makeup artists had taken my place and wonder if I'd made the right decision. My FOMO was real. I had worked long and hard to establish myself, to make it into the club, and now I felt left out. I knew it wasn't personal. That's just how the business worked. I could be the top choice for the photographers and the biggest magazines, but the second I wasn't available, they hired someone else, and I never knew if I'd get the call again. But when I asked myself if I would have rather been on a shoot than at home with my husband, I knew the answer. I still loved my work. I was still competitive. I still drove myself to improve. I just wanted to do it on my own terms.

Meanwhile, the economy and the real estate market crashed and there went most of Steven's income. He told me he was going to find a regular job in New York. I replied, "That's the stupidest thing I ever heard you say." Steven often tells people this is the greatest thing I ever said to him. I couldn't imagine the most independent and brilliant man I'd ever met, in a suit and tie, carrying a briefcase to some random office, for a job that didn't bring him joy.

Instead, he went to law school. We knew it would make life harder, at least for a little while, but it was the right decision. He passed three bars in one week, and though he never ended up practicing law, his law degree gave him the skills, knowledge, and ability to read contracts and deal with lawyers, which would eventually change our life and my business.

At the time, I put more pressure on myself to earn money. My agent would call with two offers: four days with *Glamour* at $150 a day, or six weeks with Lord & Taylor at $500 per day. Before, I might have chosen editorial work for less money because it was cooler and more fun. I tortured myself making these choices (I still do), but I began taking the higher-paying catalog work more regularly.

Catalog work had its benefits. The shoots usually lasted at least a week, sometimes longer, so I only had to schlep my heavy makeup bag once and could leave it there at the studio. The shoots usually ended at five o'clock because clients didn't want to pay hair, makeup, stylists, and models overtime. Catalog shoots were much easier and had a more laid-back style. I could walk in with my hair in a scrunchie and not worry about being judged. The makeup depended on the clothes being advertised. I'd never have to do a 1960s Jackie O pale lip or a painted face full of shocking neon colors. I just had to make the models look normal and pretty. It was nice, cushy work.

Around this time, my agent called with the job offer of a lifetime: a Ralph Lauren campaign for three weeks in Bali at my top advertising rate. These were the same people doing *Vogue* covers and every other fabulous editorial. I couldn't believe it. I was excited and panicked. I was also pregnant and couldn't imagine myself so far away from Steven, and for so long. I obsessed over the offer. What should I do? I'm sure I drove Steven crazy. We could have definitely used the money, but eventually I turned it down. At the time it was incredibly painful to let that opportunity go, but you know the old saying: when one door closes, another opens. Because I hadn't scheduled the Bali trip, I was able to take an editorial shoot that would open the door of a lifetime.

Perfect for blondes or those who favor just a touch of subtle color. Ideal for day or relaxed weekend wear.		SOFT SALMON PINK	**1**
A beautiful, natural color to wear alone. Use also to blend and tone down lip color that's too intense.		LIGHT BEIGE	**2**
Bobbi's personal favorite. This sophisticated shade lends itself beautifully to day or evening wear...let your style dictate.		DEEP RAISIN	**3**
A very natural skintone color, this is a perfect complement to all complexions. Its' subtle sophistication is ideal for day or for night.		ROSY BROWN	**4**
A hint of brown makes this a perfect rose for all skintones.		BROWNISH ROSE	**5**
Pink becomes sophisticated with a hint of brown. A very 90's way to wear pink.		THE NEW CLASSIC PINK	**6**
A truly wearable, toned down orange that brings distinctive style to the lips.		THE NEW ORANGE	**7**
A great favorite with models, this dark stain color looks especially good on those with darker complexions. A very modern, stylish color that makes a strong statement.		BLACK BERRY	**8**
A great look for all skintones, it's a sensational color for redheads and brunettes.		BURNT ORANGE	**9**
A modern, 90's way to wear red. The right red!		THE NEW CLASSIC RED	**10**

CHAPTER THIRTEEN

REINVENTING LIPSTICK

The shoot was with *Self* magazine. The theme was "makeup shopping downtown with a makeup artist." Though I was pregnant I still dressed like I always did, in a miniskirt, tights, and clogs. I took the magazine crew to a few makeup artist stores, and finally to Kiehl's pharmacy. Kiehl's was a destination—an independently owned, cool store, stuffed with health and beauty products you couldn't find anywhere else. I spent the downtime between shots in conversation with Steven, the on-site chemist. He had a little kiosk at the Kiehl's counter called Steven Cosmetics, with a couple of lipsticks. I opened a few and tried them on my hand. I liked them. Most lipsticks on the market at the time were greasy and smelled bad. They reminded me of the heavily perfumed lipstick that my mother used, the ones where you would have to apply several layers to get some color. Steven's lipsticks were dense, creamy, and scentless. You'd only need to swipe your bottom lip, smack your lips together, and voilà.

"Wow, these are nice," I said.

"I made them," Steven said.

"Really? I've always wanted to make a lipstick," I said. "What I want, you can't buy. I've been mixing and blending my own for years."

"Show me," he said.

I had my makeup kit with me, so I took out a taupe eye pencil, pink cream blush, and a lip balm and mixed the lipstick. I put it on my hand, then on my lips.

"I can make that," he said.

He took my materials, made a prototype, and mailed it to me. It came really close to what I wanted, but it wasn't perfect. I asked for changes. After a few back-and-forths, we nailed it.

"We can sell this," he said.

Why not?

We agreed to sell it for fifteen dollars and split the proceeds. He would produce the lipstick, and I would market, sell, and mail it. Nothing was in writing. I wasn't thinking about starting a business. This was just my little side hustle, before the term became popular. We started with one color, my color: I called it Brown. Soon, I realized not everyone likes this color and people have so many unique lip colors that we needed different tones. I made what I considered the perfect number of colors: ten. I numbered them one to ten and gave each a normal-sounding name. Nothing like Cherries in the Snow. No nonsense. Just a lipstick wardrobe anyone could use, with colors that either looked like lips or you could blend and mix together to create a multitude of options. I kept it simple:

SALMON

BEIGE

RAISIN

BROWN

ROSE

PINK

ORANGE

BLACKBERRY

BURNT RED

RED

I started selling them to friends, models, teachers, and women I met in the park. I didn't have boxes, so I put them in manila envelopes and mailed them. I soon realized I needed to include the ingredients, so I printed them on a card and slipped it inside the envelopes. I thought I'd be able to make some grocery money.

The colors of most lipstick brands required women to wear a face full of makeup to look good, but these lipsticks matched the natural color of lips or were muted colors that flattered the skin tone and could be worn on their own. Makeup-free makeup. It just made sense to me.

Now when I packed my kit for a shoot, I made sure to include a ziplock bag of the new lipsticks. They became my go-to tools. The models, photographers, and editors saw how good these lipsticks looked and felt and began buying them. I took orders, just like I once did as a kid in my basement jewelry store. Soon, I had a business: I took the orders; Steven the chemist made the lipstick; and Steven the husband helped track the orders, mailing them out in generic envelopes. He knew what needed to get done. We were partners. My sister-in-law Bryna kept our books. Soon we were selling a few hundred lipsticks every month.

One day, while having lunch with my friend Lesley Seymour, then beauty editor at *Glamour* magazine, I told her about my new lipstick project.

"Can I write about it?" she said.

"Why would you?" I asked, not knowing much about PR or marketing.

"I think people would love to read about it," she answered.

She wrote about the lipsticks and told people how to buy them. Overnight we got bombarded with orders. Now I had more than a side hustle. I had a small business and a growing knowledge about the power of public relations and marketing.

CHAPTER FOURTEEN

WORKING MOM

On May 4, 1990, I became a mother. This gave new meaning to the phrase "figure it out." Like many mothers at the time, I read *What to Expect When You're Expecting*. But after baby Dylan was born, I needed a book called *What Do I Do Now?* It didn't exist. I couldn't believe how amazing and exhausting it all was. It was just Steven and me doing what we always do: figuring it out. Prevailing wisdom said when the baby cries at night, let him cry it out until he puts himself back to sleep, and keep him in his crib, not your bed. Instead of crying it out, Dylan threw up all over the crib. So much for prevailing wisdom. We let him sleep in bed with us and we got some sleep.

Dylan was a tiny human but also somehow mature, independent, stubborn, and demanding—so much so that when I went to therapy feeling out of control, my therapist reminded me that I was actually the one in charge. Neither of our parents lived near us, so we hired a nanny for the days when I went back to work. Our first nanny, Maria, didn't speak a word of English. She was the cousin of our friend's nanny. She didn't have any references, and we never thought of doing a background check. When she walked in the door, opened her arms, and asked to hold the baby, she was so natural and loving that we hired her on the spot. She ended up staying with us for years and became part of our family. It just worked out. I still can't understand how she did it. I would come home from work— Dylan had gone to the park with friends, been fed, napped, and been bathed. Maria had cooked dinner and done laundry, and the house was clean. When I was home—not even close. Toys askew—me exhausted and with dinner to make and a kitchen to clean.

My new normal became many sleepless nights, followed by mornings commuting to work, and somehow pumping enough milk in between to keep the baby fed. Maria was a huge help. Not only did she care for Dylan, but when I came home, the house was perfect, dinner was on the table, and we had a clean, happy baby.

I put a lot of pressure on myself, not just professionally but also physically. I always struggled with my body image, and having had a child didn't help. My fantasy was that I would deliver my baby, put my jeans back on, and look amazing pushing the stroller. That didn't happen. It took me a year to get my weight almost back to normal.

Photo shoots were treacherous for a new mom. I was surrounded by an endless array of pasta, bread, and cookies. I'd stare at them, drooling, and hear my mother's voice in my head: You can't eat that. Working with supermodels didn't help me to feel better about myself either.

I learned of fad diets at work—each one with a different promised miraculous result. The can't-fail cleanse, the new and improved routine, the life-changing program. I'd go from one to another totally believing each one until I realized it didn't work and then moving on to something new. Like my mother, I would try anything—water cleanses, supplements, only fruit until lunch—to look and feel better.

I actually thought there must be a simple answer, a magic pill. I remember on one of our first dates, Steven and I went to a party in the city where I met a man selling metal swizzle sticks, claiming they ionized water and would fix bad digestion. Excited to improve my digestion, I found Steven.

"Can I have fifty bucks?" I said.

"What for?"

I told him about the metal swizzle stick.

He gave me the money, but he still laughs at me for it.

I was exhausted, but I was also determined to keep my career moving forward. My catalog work continued, and I also still got the occasional booking for editorial work. But now I could afford to be more picky, to press for details I previously felt were off-limits, before I accepted a job. "Who's shooting? Who are the models? Where is it?" My choices had consequences, so I became more exacting.

Having a child strengthened my resolve to say no. When I did say yes, I sometimes brought my family with me. Two weeks after Dylan was born, I was lead makeup artist for Adrienne Vittadini's fashion show in New York City, and Adrienne held Dylan while I applied makeup to her models. We had worked together so many times she was like family.

In retrospect, bringing a newborn to work wasn't the best choice. Dylan wasn't fully vaccinated, and I had to stop working to nurse him on command. He was a grazer, and I was not a scheduler. I was also learning how to maneuver the baby gear. Every night, I went home beyond exhausted, but that didn't stop me from saying yes to more jobs in more locations. Steven made much of this possible. He could study law from anywhere, he loved to travel, and he would watch the baby while I worked. Nothing ever fazed him.

I was straddling two worlds.

It all crystallized for me one day in 1990 when I got the chance to work with Francesco Scavullo, a well-known fashion photographer. Among his many achievements, Francesco shot the infamous *Cosmopolitan* centerfold picture of a nude Burt Reynolds and the movie poster for Barbara Streisand's *A Star Is Born*, and he discovered Gia Carangi, often called the first supermodel.

Careerwise, this was a big deal. Scavullo was an icon. His photographs were glamorous, and he usually worked with makeup artists like Way Bandy who were painters. I'm not sure why Francesco booked me (and would continue to book me). I had a suspicion that things were changing in the fashion industry, and maybe someone on his team advised him to modernize with a new beauty team. I was getting known for my clean, fresh style, and he hired me to do my thing, but he always wanted me to take it up a notch. It was new for him and for me, but I felt comfortable because he was so welcoming and kind. He encouraged me to add more drama while still keeping it fresh.

At the end of our first shoot, he asked me if I would want to join him and a friend for drinks and dinner. He was expecting the French fashion designer Jean Paul Gaultier. Gaultier at that time was perhaps the most famous, most controversial haute couture designer in the world. He designed the iconic cone bra for Madonna (the girl from my dance class) on her Blond Ambition World Tour.

I never cared about fame, but here I was in a room with two living legends. Pinch me. Most people in my position would have done anything to go to dinner with them, but I already had plans with my husband to take Dylan to the park. Like a scene in a movie, Steven showed up to the studio, carrying Dylan in his arms, wearing a horizontal-striped shirt. I looked back and forth, from Gaultier in his self-designed striped shirt to my husband in his Brooks Brothers striped shirt and baby Dylan in his striped T-shirt, and I thought: *Bobbi, pick a door.* I left Francesco's studio with an apology for not being able to join them and went to the park with Steven and Dylan.

These choices were hard to make, but they also created new opportunities. Prioritizing my family put me in a position to understand the challenges of working moms. Hanging at the park with other moms and their nannies gave me a chance to study regular women, to see the differences in their skin tones, to understand what they wore, what they wanted, what they liked, and what they needed. They became my new focus group. I realized that as working moms, we're overloaded and always on the run. We need makeup that is easy, multipurpose, and simple to apply without a need to touch up, because we usually have to put it on in the car while hustling from one place to another. I began to think of makeup as a solution to issues real women face. I wanted to create that solution.

CHAPTER FIFTEEN

THE BRAND

With a baby and a new business, I was busier than ever. I'd run from job to job with bags of outfit changes and my makeup kit. I was in my early thirties, excited, and open-minded. I pushed myself, and soon I found another freelance gig: to be the expert makeup artist for Aziza eye shadow. A PR firm offered me the opportunity and I took it to make some extra money, and it sounded interesting. It didn't require too much work, and I became the brand's spokesperson. I would visit the editors at all the fashion magazines, show them Aziza's products, and teach them how to apply it for different eyes. This came with two advantages: it got my name in magazines ("Makeup artist Bobbi Brown says . . ."), which helped establish me as a beauty expert, and it gave me a chance to meet all the beauty editors. I became an influencer before there was a word for that.

Roz, the woman who hired me at the PR firm, became a friend. Steven and I had many dinners with her and her husband, Ken, who worked in cosmetics, and we spent several weekends with them at their house in the Hamptons. We were friends, and like-minded couples. True story: Early on, Ken told us his parents had bought a new house in Hollywood, Florida. "That's funny," I said, "my mother just sold her house there." As it turned out, his parents had bought my mother's house.

Roz was a small, very fit Scottish woman. Where I wore jeans and a T-shirt, my hair in a ponytail, and little makeup, she wore fitted sweaters and Italian designer pants, with the perfect hair, the perfect high heels, and the perfect makeup. She was tough as nails, and adamant about always being right.

One night in the summer of 1990, Roz and Ken invited Steven and me to a cocktail party on Park Avenue. I don't remember much about the party, but I'll never forget arriving, gift in hand, and meeting the hostess, Alison Rose. I introduced myself and thanked her for inviting me.

"Happy to have you," she said. "I love your work."

"Thank you!" I said, surprised she had heard of me. "What do you do?"

"I'm a cosmetics buyer at Bergdorf Goodman," she said.

I didn't expect that.

"That's so interesting," I said. "I have a line of lipsticks I sell out of my house."

"Tell me about it."

I gave Alison my spiel: the ten colors based on natural lip tones, the special formula, the simple names.

"That's so cool!" she said. "We should sell them at Bergdorf."

"Huh? What?"

Bergdorf Goodman was the most elegant, fashionable, chic luxury department store in the world. To have them even consider stocking my everyday-woman line was incredible, so I could hardly believe it when Alison called several days later with an offer to sell my line at her store. The offer came from Alison, though, not from her bosses. A few days after that, while working on a Saks catalog shoot and showing the crew what I was working on, they said, "No, not Bergdorf's! You should pitch us!" Later, I got a message from Alison on my answering machine.

"I'm so sorry," she said, "they think we have too much makeup on the counter already. We can't take your lipstick after all." I was crushed. But I called her back and said, "No problem. Saks wants it." That wasn't entirely true—Saks had expressed interest the same way Bergdorf had, but it hadn't been approved. I was dealing on instinct, the way Papa Sam did when he got $2,000 from a restaurant to open his car dealership. "Give me a minute—let me call you back," Alison said. A few minutes later, I had a deal with Bergdorf Goodman.

The problem was, I didn't have a real company yet. Steven and I invited Roz and Ken to our house and discussed becoming partners. Roz was great at copywriting and PR, and she was uber-confident. Ken worked in the beauty industry. It just made sense. Now we needed a name. Someone said, "Why don't we just call it Bobbi Brown?" That was it. The brand became Bobbi Brown Essentials, a makeup line for real women, designed by a makeup artist.

Next we needed a package for the product and a concept for how we'd display it at Bergdorf Goodman. From a catalog, we picked a simple black rectangular lipstick case with a gold band that reminded me of Chanel. That became our look. When it came to designing our tester unit—the base that would hold the lipsticks on the makeup counter—Steven said, "I hate those cheap plastic ones. Let's make ours out of stone." He had one of his contractors do just that.

Selling lipstick at department stores required inventory, which meant we needed an upgrade from the ziplock bag with a handful of tubes inside. We needed to scale up. Steven the chemist couldn't meet the demand (and, frankly, a fifty-fifty split wasn't a business model anyway), which meant I had to find a new manufacturer and hope they could produce exactly what I wanted. I made many calls but couldn't find anyone, until one day, riding the elevator at the apartment we kept on Fourth Avenue, I said hello to the woman next to me. We made small talk, and I asked, "What do you do?" As it turned out, she worked in a cosmetics lab in Queens. I took her card and ended up hiring her lab to make my lipstick.

The new lab had to re-create the formula, which required a lot of back and forth. They'd send me a tester, and I'd send it back with a note: too greasy. Another one: too dry. Another one: I don't like the slip (how it feels gliding across the lip). I couldn't sell an inferior product to Bergdorf. I had to re-create the formula of the originals. I asked to speak to the chemist making the formula, a very nice guy named Dave. I kept trying to explain to him what I wanted, but he didn't understand. "You're trying it on your hand, Dave," I said. "Please, try it on your lips." It took a bit of convincing to get this dude to wear lipstick, but as soon as he did, he said, "I see exactly what you mean." The next tester was perfect. We were ready to introduce Bobbi Brown Essentials to the world. In the same year, I had a new baby and a new company to launch.

The release was set for February 1991. Invitations were sent to friends, family, colleagues, and the beauty press. But a few weeks before the opening, the lipstick cases arrived from China, and they didn't fit. The tops kept falling off the cases. I had a massive freakout. "We're never going to make this launch," I told Steven, spiraling deeper and deeper into panic. "It's going to be over before it even starts." Steven calmed me down. Somehow we were able to convince the catalog to rush ship new cases, which they did, just in time for the launch.

On opening day at Bergdorf Goodman, I wore a khaki-green Armani blazer that my father bought me for my thirtieth birthday (I had picked it out). It had these really big shoulder pads and was way too long for my size, but it was my power jacket. I wanted to look like a professional woman. My dad and sister flew in. My sisters-in-law came with flowers. I brought baby Dylan, dressed in a little motorcycle jacket. The room was filled with press, beauty editors, models, photographers, and industry types. It was a mixture of fashion cool, family, and friends.

Standing outside, I gazed at our Fifth Avenue window display. It was an amazing feeling. Inside, the room was buzzing. The display was on a table in the middle of a department store, because we didn't have enough product to fill a counter. It didn't matter. I was thrilled to just be in the store. If they had asked me to set up in the ladies' room, I would have said yes.

As the day progressed and customers shuffled in and out, a funny thing happened: some people bought all ten colors. Most of that was probably the competition trying to figure out *what is this?* After all, who had ever heard of a makeup artist designing her own line of lipstick? We hoped to sell one hundred lipsticks the first month. Instead, we sold one hundred the first day.

I left Bergdorf Goodman elated, having no idea what I had just started. I still saw myself as a makeup artist with a side hustle. Steven and I took Dylan back home to Montclair, to our real life. Time to feed and bathe my child, cook dinner, and get ready for the next day.

But my life and work were evolving. There was Manhattan Bobbi, the chic, hip, urban makeup artist with a line of lipsticks in Bergdorf Goodman, and there was Montclair Bobbi, the mother and wife with mommy-and-me classes to attend and diapers to change. Back when I was struggling with the decision to leave the *Vogue* world in favor of my family, I didn't know I could create a life in which I got to have both. But now I knew. It took luck, determination, and an incredible partner to navigate it all. Steven was in law school, acquiring real estate properties for development, and managing the new cosmetics company. It was crazy and exhilarating. By age thirty-three, I was a makeup artist, wife, mother, and businesswoman with the beginning of a brand.

BOBBI BROWN
essentials

You are cordially invited to meet
leading makeup artist
Bobbi Brown

at the exclusive launch of her
new line of lipsticks --
BOBBI BROWN ESSENTIALS

on Wednesday, February 20th
12:30 pm to 1:30 pm

CHAPTER SIXTEEN

ESSENTIALS

As our business began to take off, Roz still worked her full-time PR job, and I still waited for my agent to tell me who had called to book me for what shoot. But near the end of 1991, we started making enough money from lipstick sales to take salaries. Roz quit her job and became the president of Bobbi Brown Essentials. We rented a small office on Park Avenue and invited the press. I'll never forget the day we got a visit from *Vogue* beauty editor Shirley Lord. She was chic, very respected, very beloved, but also very intimidating. In later years, I'd see her at parties and bar mitzvahs in Montclair—her husband's son lived in town—and get to know her, but a visit from her in the early days was like a visit from the queen. "Oh my God, Shirley is coming! We have to get ready!" She came to the office and said, "Who's bankrolling this?" She couldn't understand how we were doing it. She wrote about the company in the beauty pages of *Vogue*, and kept writing about us. That was another moment of arrival.

While Roz changed jobs, I just added another job to my list. I spent my days dashing in and out of the office, working on ideas for the brand and keeping up with my editorial magazine work. My magazine work was good for the brand, plus it still really excited me. I loved working with people at the top of their game. I continued to bring Dylan to shoots, and when I didn't have help, I'd just hand him to whoever was around. I have many pictures of my son in the arms of stunning models. I was selective about what jobs I took and who I was going to work with. I might not take a job with Steven Klein, who would be shooting until 4 a.m., but I would work with Walter Chin, who had three kids of his own, understood what I was going through, and was okay with me leaving at five in the evening.

After a decade in the industry, I had relationships and I had attention. Roz and I would put together our press kit for the season and pitch the magazines, weeklies, national newspapers, and regionals. The best press came from stories that mentioned "makeup by Bobbi Brown." As more and more fashion editors asked me to appear in their magazines, people on the street would stop me to say, "I love your lipstick." It was starting to catch on. Editors called with shoot opportunities, and I'd run to do them. I had already become known as a makeup artist, but now with my own line, I was becoming a beauty expert.

At Fashion Week in early 1992, I noticed a shift. As I worked on the models, I also had to field questions from the press: "Bobbi, what are we going to see this season?" "Bobbi, what's the trend?" I never knew the trend, and I certainly never followed the trend. But I knew the makeup that we were launching, and that became what I'd put forward as the trend: "This season is all about nude lipstick . . ."

The more press I did, the better the lipsticks sold. Bergdorf Goodman couldn't believe the excitement at our makeup counter. Burt Tansky, Bergdorf's president, gave me so much support. He was a real merchant, a Papa Sam type who had worked his way up, and he inspired his employees to follow his lead. Having his support meant everything. One day, he came down to the makeup department, looked at the crowds of people waiting to buy lipstick, scratched his head, and said, "We need more products."

Why not?

Since we already had a line of lipsticks, it made sense to make a lip pencil. In those days, women would draw a darker line around their lips with a pencil and then fill the rest in with lipstick, and I thought it looked fake. What if I made a lip pencil where you couldn't see the difference between the pencil and the lipstick? Also, my technique was different. I discovered that if you put the lipstick on first, then the pencil, it was easier and looked more natural. I taught this technique to the makeup artist behind the counter and demonstrated how to select the right shade of lip pencil. Instead of selling one product, we now sold two.

Next, we created eye shadows. My ideal eye shadow was flat and dense, not dry and crumbly. I had a unique technique on how to apply it. It was not how the magazines did it, not how the painterly artists did it. Many makeup artists had the skill to blend a dark eye shadow for a look most normal women could not re-create at home. I did not have this skill, but I knew how I wanted women to look. I figured out a way to layer eye shadow from light to dark to achieve the same effect. What if I made an eye shadow you didn't have to blend? What if it came out of the package just looking right? My best talent was that I wasn't a skilled artist. This forced me to rely on what I could do, and that's what spoke to everyday women.

We hired someone to work in product development. I'd tell her what I wanted and she'd tell the lab or the chemist. If I wasn't completely satisfied with the product, I tweaked it until I was. Sometimes, after many rounds of telephone, I would go to the lab and show the chemists what I wanted. I think in pictures, not words.

My work style was not for everyone. Including Roz. I'm visual and creative and think outside the box. We were two very different people trying to work together toward the same goal. The more we succeeded, the further apart we grew. She was fancy and wanted the company to appeal to the glitzy uptown clientele. I was simple and wanted the company to demystify that glitzy world of beauty. Many of my ideas were geared toward working mothers because that was my life. Every night I'd come home exhausted, change Dylan's diaper and clean him with baby wipes, put him to bed, then go into my bathroom and take my makeup off with a face cleanser and a washcloth. What if I made a makeup wipe with a cleanser to take the makeup off in one step? I told Roz the idea.

She was not on board. We didn't do it.

Women had to buy so many different creams, one for under the eyes, one for the neck, one for the body. What if I created one cream that could be used all over? "Women need different creams," Roz said. We didn't do it.

Things got worse when I heard she was contradicting my instructions. I'd have a concept for the season—the colors, the names, the marketing ideas—and would convey it to the team. Later, when I saw that the product wasn't what I asked for, I'd get upset at my team, until they explained: "Roz told us to do it this way." I usually got my way in the end, but this was an aggravating way to operate.

All that said, we never would have been as successful without Roz and Ken. We probably wouldn't even have been able to build the company without the skills they brought to the endeavor. Roz was strong-willed, determined, exacting, and unapologetic. I was naive and excitable and eager to do something different from the norm.

Looking back, I realize I could have done things better. I had never started a company before. I didn't know how important it is to have clearly defined roles in a partnership. I cared about details, but I didn't care about charts, graphs, and numbers. I wanted to know about everything, but I didn't want to be in charge of everything. That's why I partnered with Roz. Ultimately, I cared most about creating products and finding new, interesting ways to market them. Those products carried my name, my face, and my reputation. I had to be certain I approved of them before they went to market. I had a clear vision, and I expected my team to execute it. I didn't recognize that might conflict with Roz's sense of her role and responsibility. Unfortunately, I never expressed this to Roz. I didn't have the confidence to deal with the issues head-on. Instead, I held it in until I got home and exploded to Steven until he calmed me down. I suppose we all could have handled it better.

By the end of 1991, I was running as fast as I could, developing new products, booking magazine shoots, raising Dylan—and I was pregnant again. It was crazy, and I loved it. I had spent so many years thinking I wasn't enough, wanting to prove myself. When I discovered how capable I was, I said, *Okay, watch me*—not to my parents or peers; to myself.

We continued adding products, but Bergdorf didn't have a counter for us in the cosmetics department, so they offered us something that seemed random: a counter in the handbag section, right outside the makeup department. A lot of traditional companies would have said, "No, we'll wait." I thought, *Why not?*

It ended up being a great decision. It made the brand seem more special. Sales were strong and Bergdorf's sister store, Neiman Marcus, asked to carry the line.

Why not?

CHAPTER SEVENTEEN

WORK/LIFE BALANCE

In August 1992, baby Dakota (Cody) joined his brother Dylan. Two sons meant two feedings, two diapers, two car seats, two of everything. Steven and I had already been in the trenches, so even though the workload doubled, we handled it. With the first kid, if the pacifier fell on the floor, we sterilized it. With the second one, we'd just wipe it off and put it back in his mouth.

My career had become incredibly busy, but my family was always my focus. Steven and I were equal partners in everything. He was my go-to business coach, and we organically subdivided our home life. It wasn't always easy. We had moments of stress and chaos, but somehow we made it work. He was always there to talk me off the ledge or to help me calm down when I lost it. He stepped in to help with the kids when I had last-minute work obligations, and in return I respected his personal time for exercise, sports, and his growing business.

Dakota was an easy baby from the start. He was happy, active, and adorable with his snow-white hair and piercing blue eyes. It was no problem if I forgot his toys—he was happy with his toes or an empty cup. What a gift for this working mom.

Of course, with two kids and packed schedules, we had to work hard to find time for each other. We still do. Our anniversary is like a national holiday to us. I take the day off. And, like any couple, we had—and still have—our fights. Even after all these years, they're usually about me not being present or me being buggy because I am swept up in everything I have to do. But we were cementing the foundation of respect, love, and trust that has kept us deeply in love for thirty-seven years and counting.

When we launched at Neiman Marcus in 1991, I was obligated to show up for personal appearances in stores around the country. Again, I didn't look forward to traveling without my family, but Steven was more than happy to join with the boys, so I was able to have my work life and not miss out on my family life.

These trips were usually whirlwinds. The night before, I'd run around the house, throwing things into suitcases. "We need bottles! We need pajamas! We need diapers!" We'd fly to Texas or Florida or California, check into a hotel, set up two cribs, and collapse into bed.

The next day, I'd get up early, get a blowout, put on my makeup, and start the press junket. I'd be interviewed for local television news, fashion magazines, and newspapers. Then I'd head to the store for personal appearances. While customers sat with one of our makeup artists, I'd walk around, say hello, and make color suggestions. I also trained my team so they knew what to do, and after the event, I'd be able to use them as a sounding board: "What are people looking for?" It was my market research.

It took a while for some markets to understand my style. In the early nineties, my no-makeup makeup look still conflicted with the dominant trend. When I first started traveling to Texas, for example, many customers wanted a bolder, heavily made-up style and didn't understand that a yellow foundation looked better than a pink one. We slowly broke into that market with regular makeup artist training to educate the artists behind the counter, who would then teach the customers how they could look even better by using colors that are more complementary to their skin tone. The makeup artists were always the bridges and the best ambassadors for the brand.

Meanwhile, I was creating my own path in more ways than one. At the time, professional women were expected to leave their family life at home. I, on the other hand, never tried to hide that I was a working mother. I showed up to Neiman Marcus one time not knowing I had baby spit-up running down my back. Often, by the end of these events I'd be leaking milk all over my blouse because I hadn't nursed the baby in so long. Then Steven would come in with the strollers, and the kids would come running up to me. No one at Neiman Marcus had ever seen anything like it.

Even with the help from Steven and the team, the four to five hours I'd spend with customers drained me. By the time they were over, I wanted to lie on the floor in a ball, but I couldn't. I had to be on for the customers and for the makeup artists who had been waiting for me. Instead of saying "I can't do this," I thought, *How can I do this better?* I made adjustments. I shortened the appearances (though they'd still run over) and started taking a head makeup artist around with me who could answer questions from the customers so I could communicate my vision for natural makeup to the public and the press. I started bringing a bag of snacks and a bottle of water to fuel me better to do my job.

In early 1992, I received an offer for a shoot in Florida with Niki Taylor, who had just become the face of CoverGirl. She was a big deal. We scheduled a much-needed family vacation around this shoot, but just before we left, baby Cody got an ear infection and the doctor said he couldn't fly. Crushed, I prepared to cancel the shoot and our vacation. Steven had a solution. I was to take the plane with Dylan, while he took a train to Florida with baby Cody. A dad traveling with a two-month-old in an overnight coach for twenty-four hours? What a man! The shoot went well and we had a wonderful vacation.

Still, these pressures continued to build, and so did the tension between me and Roz. Added to all the other stress in my life, the situation at work was becoming unbearable. I'd cry when I got home at night and pour out my troubles to Steven. "Let them win the battle," he'd say. "We'll win the war." I didn't understand what he meant.

We hired a business therapist to mediate our relationship. I knew her from Montclair. She would have a separate session with me and one with Roz, and then we'd have a session together. It didn't help. One day, during a session with me, she said, "Have you ever thought about taking an antianxiety medication, and maybe you'll be calmer about what Roz is doing?" That was my last session with her.

Despite all these challenges, the company was thriving. It was an intense and exciting time. I was full speed ahead. I didn't know where all of this was going. I didn't know what to compare it to. But by the end of 1994, three years after launching the brand, we were the top-selling line in Bergdorf Goodman and Neiman Marcus. We were onto something special.

Billboard – Dallas, TX

Life Captured

shot on Lake Michigan in Chicago
by Jeffrey Licata

CHAPTER EIGHTEEN

WHAT IF/ WHY NOT

I've always been open-minded. I see possibilities, not obstacles—you can tell that by now. Rarely do I have a grand plan. I just follow what interests me. At crucial moments in my life, I have always asked two questions: *What if?* And *Why not?* That's how I ended up at Emerson College (*What if* I studied makeup?), that's how I landed in New York (*Why not* try to make it in the big city?), and that's how I created my own line of lipstick (*What if* I made the makeup I always wanted but couldn't find?).

I didn't have a mind for math, science, or literature, but I've somehow always figured out how to achieve my goals. It's a combination of Aunt Alice's common sense, Papa Sam's relentlessness, my dad's fearless experimentation, and my mom's constant encouragement that I could do anything. I had a lot of help along the way, but help took me only so far. I had to figure it out for myself.

Figuring it out, to me, means being open to changing my mind, trying and failing and trying again. It doesn't mean never failing or accepting a failure. But often what we view as failure is actually a breeding ground for creativity.

Being quick on my feet has led to some of the biggest breakthroughs of my career as a makeup artist and an executive. For example: I was once hired to key Rachel Roy's fashion show, and Rachel wanted lipstick the color of Hershey's Kisses and espresso. I asked my assistant for my lip palette to see what I could do. "Uh-oh, I forgot to pack it," the assistant whispered. I didn't freak; I took a moment, considered my options, and said, "Hand me the eye shadow palette and the lip balm." With these tools, I created a color never seen before, not even by me. After the show, Rachel said she couldn't have imagined a more perfect color palette. Anna Wintour commented on how fabulous it looked, and *Vogue* wrote about it. As a result, I created a lipstick color called Chocolate, all because I didn't panic or quit.

PART FIVE

BE
NORMAL

CHAPTER NINETEEN

ON TOP
OF THE
WORLD

As the number one beauty brand in both Bergdorf Goodman and Neiman Marcus, we started getting requests for meetings from people wanting to invest in, or even buy, Bobbi Brown Essentials. We had no interest in selling, but we took the meetings. One of them was with the cosmetic giant Shiseido. We had a few meetings and meals, but it never went anywhere. Another came from a Dallas investment company. When we told them we were not ready to sell, they told us that they were going to find another makeup artist to re-create our model.

Next I got a call from a friend, the hairdresser Frédéric Fekkai, who said, "Leonard Lauder would like an introduction. Can I give him your number?"

Leonard is Estée Lauder's son and was then the CEO of the global empire. To most people, Estée Lauder is a brand name, something you hear on a commercial or see in a store. To me, it was a behemoth of a brand that was high-end, respected, and on top of its game. To Leonard, it was the family business. The Lauders were like American royalty, so naturally I had an out-of-body experience when Leonard invited Roz and me to his apartment for dinner with him and his wife, Evelyn. This was like an invitation to meet the king.

It was late summer 1995 when I took the elevator to the penthouse of the Lauders' Fifth Avenue apartment building and knocked on the door. I was instantly struck by how tall he was. He put his hand on my shoulder and said, "So nice to meet you." Leonard was as lovely as I could have hoped. I instantly felt comfortable, like I could say anything to him, and that never changed. He later described our meeting as "love at first sight."

Leonard and Evelyn gave us a tour of their apartment, which looked like an art gallery. Beside picture windows overlooking Central Park the walls were lined with works by Picasso, Braque, and Klimt, among other incredible art. He and Evelyn had raised their sons there, so I couldn't help but ask, "Your kids actually lived in this apartment?" He laughed and said, "It was a little messier then."

Dinner was beautiful. He had done his homework and somehow knew I liked super-healthy food. We sat on his roof eating brown rice, grilled chicken, steamed broccoli, and salad, with sorbet and fruit for dessert. We used blue bandannas for napkins. Then we sat sipping wonderful wine, watching dusk fall over the city, listening to the music of a live symphony performing in the park. Leonard told me I reminded him of his mother. Then he told me how much he admired our work and said, "You're outselling us in the stores. We can't beat you, so we thought we'd buy you."

"Thank you, but we're not looking to sell," I replied.

"What if I tell you that you could do exactly what you love, and not do any of the things you don't love?" he said. "I know what you want to do with your life. I know you want to be a mother and a wife, and I know you really want to do the creative things and not worry about the business." Leonard said the Estée Lauder corporation could help grow the brand, while giving me complete creative autonomy. By the end of this magical evening, we agreed to consider his offer. I came down the elevator starry-eyed, thinking, what just happened?

It was a number of weeks before we received Estée Lauder's official offer. We went about our lives, trying to play it cool. We didn't want to seem too eager. We had so many questions about what they'd ask of me, and my involvement—not to mention what the actual number might be.

But when the offer came, it was life changing.

Steven and Ken took the reins and handled the details. I'm not good with spreadsheets. They involved a lawyer and told me what was happening step by step.

One major catch: Estée would own my brand and my name, and I couldn't start a competing business for twenty-five years.

Steven warned me that this might be a problem, which was when I began counting on my fingers. Twenty-five plus thirty-seven equals . . . sixty-two . . . and said, "No worries, I won't want to work when I'm in my sixties."

And so, I signed, and we sold the company that was not for sale. We didn't agonize over the decision. Steven and I aren't agonizers. We make up our minds and move on. That's how we've always operated.

It wasn't just the money that convinced me. Sure, it meant I never had to work again if I didn't want to. It meant we could provide for our families. But the company meant more to me than a payout, and besides, we were doing well enough not to worry about money. I agreed to the sale because of Leonard. I knew he was the right person to learn from. He told me he'd take care of me and my brand.

That was one reason I signed the contract. There was another too. Under Leonard's leadership, I would have the freedom to create products and communicate my message, to concentrate on what mattered to me. And Leonard believed in me. He really thought I had a special talent and creative instinct. I did too. But his belief gave me confidence to really be me.

Steven and I were in Nantucket with friends, sitting on the beach with our kids, when we received the final call. Steven took it on his car phone, which was powered by the engine back then, so he had to drive around to keep the signal. I'll never forget the moment he got back and said, "The deal is done!" It was the same moment my son Dakota said for the first time ever, "I have to pee," then took off his diaper and went to the bathroom by himself. I remember looking at the back of his little three-year-old tush, marveling about my two worlds and how they existed side by side. I was a normal person who somehow had all these crazy good things happening.

We celebrated with Roz and Ken. Even though our relationship had its tough moments, we were happy and proud of our accomplishments together. But Steven and I wanted to celebrate. We weren't sure exactly what to do. We liked our house. I loved my Land Rover. We didn't lust after possessions, and we saw no reason to buy something expensive just because we could. We went from having enough money to pay our mortgage and go on a few vacations to never having to worry about money again. It felt so great, but we decided it would be even greater if our brothers and sisters didn't have to worry either. We told them that their kids' college expenses would be paid for as well.

After that I said to Steven: "We have to buy something, don't we?" So we went shopping in Manhattan at ABC Carpet, but only came home with a little stool for the boys to step on when they washed their hands and a Winnie-the-Pooh rug. On the drive home, Steven said, "What do you think of buying floor seats at the New Jersey Nets?" Why not? We called from the car. The salesman we met with remains one of our closest friends to this day. We finally found something we felt comfortable spending money on—a fun experience we could enjoy with the kids that would make us part of a community, and just a short drive from our house.

Before Steven and I were married we rented a charming one-room studio in the potato fields of Bridgehampton. It actually smelled like baked potatoes in the heat of summer. One of our small but symbolic extravagances was enjoyed at a gourmet food store in the Hamptons called Loaves & Fishes. We'd often stop at the store to buy lunch. Everything looked incredible, especially the lobster salad, which sold for more per pound than fit our budget, so we'd order an eighth of a pound and relish every bite. We told ourselves that if we ever made money, we would shop at the store and not think about the prices. On our next visit to the Hamptons, we proudly approached the counter to order our lobster salad: "We want a whole pound!"

CHAPTER TWENTY

THE WONDER YEARS

At Estée Lauder, my eyes popped open just like they did at Emerson, except now I had fifteen years of experience in makeup, a successful business, and a cosmetics giant supporting me. Before the sale, the brand was a fast car. Now I was riding a rocket ship. While I had the full support of the brand, I think Roz had a difficult time with our new partners. She left the company after a year, and we had a new interim president.

From the start, we hired a great product-development team who were as excited about working with me as I was about working with them. Leonard made the Estée Lauder labs available, and I treated them like a playground, sticking my fingers in jars of shimmers and colors, trying this, testing that, sampling the other. We ran into an early snag when someone suggested we bring our formulas in-house, instead of outsourcing to the lab we had been using, to make our lipsticks. Leonard proved to be a man of his word and said, "Absolutely not. If you change that formula, women will know and they won't want it anymore." He insisted we remain true to our brand. It was a win for us and for our supplier (I still work with them today), and it gave them a chance to work with a cosmetics giant.

I was invigorated in the corporate meetings, discussing the future and what we wanted to achieve. I liked not knowing things. I liked listening. I liked giving my opinion and discussing it with people who knew what they were doing and were open to what I had to say. I had the most fun preparing for our twice-yearly sales meetings, with our marketing and PR teams discussing "How are we going to show the collection this season?" Everything started with the editors and then trickled down to the sales staff and, ultimately, the customers. We began ideating innovative, cool, fun ways to get everyone excited and engaged.

It always started with a theme. One season was about chocolatey colors, so we came up with the idea to make a bunch of chocolate bars with Vosges, this cool, female-owned chocolate company, and to serve hot cocoa at the sales meetings. Another time we wanted to bring diamond dust and jeweled colors to life. We bought lots of rhinestone jewels for everyone to wear at meetings and in the store. It was like planning an event launch each time.

Because Bobbi Brown Essentials was the number one line at Bergdorf and Neiman, I had the freedom to bring my wild ideas to life, as well as the team to do it. Leonard often came to our big sales meetings and told my team, "I have two words for you: 'Yes, Bobbi.'" Everybody laughed because they knew what he meant. My title was chief creative officer. My job was to create. I felt liberated, engaged, and supported. He was my biggest champion.

I never struggled for ideas. If anything, I had too many. Even to this day. I find inspiration everywhere. I might look at a brick building and want to do a brick color. I love looking at food and packaging. I especially find inspiration in the colors on people's faces. Once, during a vacation in Telluride, my kids came home from skiing with bright red cheeks and chapped red lips. I came up with a color called Slopes to try to re-create that incredible red color. Also in Telluride, hiking on a breezy summer day, I looked down and saw beautiful cool stones of different colors. I made an eye palette based on the tones of the rocks and a bronzer that looked like the color of your tan after you come home from hiking.

Whenever inspiration struck, I'd call our then head of marketing Maureen and say, "I have a great idea." I loved working with Maureen. She was strong, smart, and cool and she understood me. She had kids and a husband, just like me. She knew the cosmetics business and understood my vision. When we talked, the conversation just clicked. When we first met, her corporate job required constant travel, which took her away from her family. I offered her a job as my head of marketing, and we brought the idea to corporate. They didn't feel it was a good career move for her, because technically it was a downgrade from the title she held. She decided to do it anyway. She eventually became president of Bobbi Brown Cosmetics.

After I'd discussed a new idea with Maureen, we'd get the lab to make sure the colors and textures were exactly what I wanted, then get the PR team to make sure we had a strong marketing and sales strategy, and then get the press on board. Finally, we had the sales team coordinate the rollout in stores and windows all over the world. I did this every season, every year.

It was a roller coaster, and I kept pushing and going. Steven was always there to catch me, to push me—whatever I needed. I was completely overwhelmed, always freaking out. How am I going to travel and take care of the kids and get to work and make dinner and . . . He was the calm, collected one. He'd say, "Just breathe. You're fine. We got this." At night when I'd start venting my stress while he was watching the ten o'clock *Seinfeld* rerun, he'd say, "Not now. We can talk about it tomorrow." I realized what I worried about at night was often much easier to deal with in the morning.

Our international sales kept growing, and that required travel. This was different from flying to Florida or Texas to visit a Neiman Marcus store. I still didn't want to be away from my family any more than I had to, so I'd tell them to overschedule me. Yes, I flew first-class and stayed in some of the best hotels in the world—sometimes with butlers—but I worked myself to exhaustion. Every second was booked: TV appearances, dinners, interviews, meetings, speeches.

The stress often began before I even left the house. Once, Dylan got chicken pox just before I was scheduled to go to London for a huge press junket. I sat there thinking, I can't go and I can't cancel.

Steven and I figured out that I could leave a day later if Dylan was better, but that meant I had to fly to London overnight and go directly on live television. And that's what I did.

After six hours on a plane, I landed at around five in the morning with a call time for the television appearance at seven. I barely had time to get my luggage and make it to the station, where I was whisked into hair and makeup and sent out in front of the cameras. There's a particular mixture of exhaustion and adrenaline in these moments that I have grown to know well. It's bone-chillingly painful to be that tired, but I know I have to perform or I won't have a career. Not only does the makeup have to look right on the model, I also have to look good. While I have people to support me, ultimately I am the one who has to perform. There's so much at stake, such responsibility to the company and to myself. I put my exhaustion aside and performed. Of course, I over-caffeinated to keep myself going. Then I'd get into bed at night, wired from the coffee and stress, and wonder why I couldn't sleep. It was hard, but I did it because this was more than my job; it was my calling.

After two pregnancies, the stress and travel only intensified my old issues with body image. Now in my late thirties, I had developed a much healthier relationship with food, but I hadn't yet freed myself from my mother's worldview. I still tried crazy diets, and as usual, the minute I ate something off the starvation plan, my body would blow up. I had major digestive issues. Even worse was the mental and emotional toll. I remember getting off a flight to Paris and running straight to Zara to get pants that fit me because whatever I had eaten on the plane had changed my shape. It was awful. My

PR people looked at me like, you're full of it. I put my pants on and said, "Look, these pants fit two days ago!"

I'd return home from these trips drained and have to immediately snap back into mom mode. Juggling my two worlds became increasingly challenging. I learned to surround myself with people who would help me, from assistants to creative partners. I built a team of the people I wanted to work with, the people that made me happy and helped me succeed. We became a little cliquey, and I knew this might not have been okay with people who weren't on the inside, but this was my team, and it worked for me for a long time.

Besides Steven, I also had help at home, plus a few after-school and weekend babysitters who were often teacher's assistants to high school and college kids. The same way I developed hacks to simplify makeup, I also developed hacks to simplify my home life. Dylan was always a sleepyhead. I had the hardest time waking him up in the morning, let alone getting him dressed and ready for school on time. My hack when he was young: bathe him at night, then dress him in his school clothes for bed, so when he woke up, he was ready to go. I also began to prepare breakfast the night before and set my work things in a bag by the door.

Dinner was a constant struggle. We didn't consider hiring a cook—we still liked things simple and our own way. My go-to on Sundays: I'd buy a whole roasted chicken, pasta, frozen vegetables, and Rao's marinara sauce, strip the chicken, cook the pasta, and put everything in separate glass containers that could go from the microwave to the table to the dishwasher and looked good in my glass-door refrigerator for when I came home. Instead of relying on fast food or takeout, I could throw it all in a pot and make my kids a healthy dinner in ten minutes. I was always thinking: *What do I need?* I never thought very far in the future. Just: *What's the next thing I need?*

No matter how hard it got, with Steven at my side and my posse to support me, I could do it. Plus, I was having the time of my life. These were the wonder years. I had the sense that what we were creating together—whether at work with my team or at home with my family—was magic.

CHAPTER TWENTY-ONE

THE GLORY YEARS

Working with Leonard opened up a whole new world. Besides being the king of the beauty industry, he sat on the board at the Whitney Museum of American Art, was a major benefactor to the Metropolitan Museum of Art, and counted himself a member of several elite organizations, including the Council on Foreign Relations, the President's Council of Memorial Sloan Kettering Cancer Center, and more. His social calendar sometimes became mine, which meant grand parties, galas, and soirees. Steven and I often had a seat at his table. Sometimes we felt like farmers in the big city. And yet there we were, sitting at the popular table next to the popular guy. One party, Steven was sandwiched between Helen Gurley Brown and Elizabeth Hurley, while I sat between Leonard and Hugh Grant.

It took me a while to acclimate to this stratosphere. I was not normally intimidated meeting famous people. But in this environment I wondered, *Am I wearing the right clothes? Does my hair look okay?* I wasn't confident enough that by being myself I would fit in. So I wore shoes that hurt me, and clothes that were too tight, trying to live up to my idea of what fancy was.

I went through a similar experience in my new Estée Lauder office. The GM Building on Fifth Avenue is just a few minutes' walk from our former office on Park Avenue, but it was light-years away. The building itself is imposingly tall, soaring fifty stories high. I'd show up every day and enter the huge front doors along with businesspeople dressed in business clothes and business shoes, carrying their briefcases, ready to do business.

Estée Lauder had its own dress code. Women had to wear pants and a blazer or a dress, with closed-toe shoes and stockings. Most women wore high heels, and you could hear them clicking on the marble floors that lined the hallways. That wasn't me. I dressed like an artist: jeans, sneakers, a cool sweater, messy hair. No one at Lauder said, "Bobbi, you have to dress like this," but I felt the pressure to fit in, so I conformed, or at least I tried to, but it never felt comfortable.

Even worse, my corporate outfit only made my crazy days crazier. A typical day looked like this: I'd drop the kids at school in

Montclair, head to the city for an early-morning meeting, rush to a photo shoot downtown, then back to the GM building for more meetings, then back to Montclair to get the kids home and fed and bathed (and clean up the pile of shoes by the front door), then sometimes attend an evening party back in the city or a back-to-school event in Montclair. Before leaving the house, I would shove four different outfits in a bag, because I never knew what role I might have to play. I needed my corporate outfit for work, but I couldn't wear that to a *Vogue* shoot. I'd change in the bathroom and put on my jeans, T-shirt, and sneakers before heading downtown. Then I would change once again if I had an event in the city. I had a uniform for every role.

I did this for more than a decade, until I figured out how to hack my uniform: navy or black pants (machine washable, no dry cleaning), or dark jeans, a white shirt and blazer, and loafers or platforms, depending on where I was going. But it took a lot of experience, wisdom, and confidence to get there.

My core beauty philosophy never changed. I cared about making great products for women. The business was growing and consumers were responding, and I was still figuring it all out. But as the business grew, so did the pressure. I used to quietly walk around the streets of New York, but now someone would often stop me and say, "Oh my God, do you know who you look like?" I also got a lot of: "Wow, I thought you were taller." I began to feel the scrutiny at public events, especially at Fashion Week. I would spend the week before doing a cleanse and starving myself because I knew I'd have a bunch of cameras following me around, photographing me from every angle, and I wanted to look my best. I had to ask myself: *What outfit will make me look slim? What would be flattering on me?* I knew these pictures would appear in newspapers and on TV all over the world, and with my fine-tuned eye for detail, this caused a lot of unnecessary stress.

It was a challenge to come down after these events. I'll never forget after one Fashion Week when I met Steven at the Harvard Club in Midtown, Manhattan. Earlier that day, people were in my face—*Bobbi, what's the latest trend? Bobbi, can I take a picture? Bobbi, can we get a quote? Bobbi, Bobbi.* I got on the elevator at the club and a woman said, "Are you Bobbi?"

"How do you know me?" I asked.

"I don't," she said. "I asked if you were going to the lobby."

Humbling.

CHAPTER TWENTY-TWO

DOWNTOWN BOBBI BROWN

A few years after I joined Estée Lauder, I was at lunch with the then CEO Fred Langhammer when he said to me, "Bobbi, your business is flat. What do you suggest we do about it?"

I was floored. "Fred," I said, "why do we have to keep growing like we have been?"

I think smoke came out of his ears. He explained that more revenue meant a healthy business.

"I have an idea," I said. "Why don't we cut the unnecessary expenses, and our numbers will be much better?"

That didn't convince him.

I started to think seriously about what more I could do to make the business more profitable. I had noticed these cool and relaxed brands starting to pop up, like Stila Cosmetics, founded by makeup artist Jeanine Lobell, who packaged her products in innovative cardboard containers. That's how I'd always seen my company, but that wasn't how we operated in our corporate setting. I told Fred that I wanted to move out of the GM Building, where we were trying to conform to rules that didn't encourage creativity and innovation, find a loft downtown, and relax the culture in the office. I'd also replace the acting president of Bobbi Brown Cosmetics. Roz and the company had parted ways during our first year at Lauder, and we had a new president who was very nice but, in my view at least, didn't quite fit the brand's ethos. I suggested I'd elevate my head of marketing, Maureen.

"Okay," Fred said. "You've got a year. Show me what you can do."

I got right to work. We moved to an office on Broadway, in SoHo, and immediately felt more at home, liberated from the corporate confines of the GM Building. Gone were the suits and briefcases, replaced by a relaxed dress code of jeans and sneakers. The office also featured a few dogs.

It was the best of both worlds. I got to create a cool, unique environment, but I also had the juggernaut of Estée Lauder behind me. All my years of hard work had come to fruition. I had invented the no-makeup makeup look, developed products for it, and proved it could succeed with women all over the world. Now I truly owned it.

As a makeup artist who was imagining a brand for women, I tried to make everything simpler and better. I'd always thought the brushes that came in palettes were too skinny and flat, making the product difficult to apply. I'd go to the art store, buy a bunch of paintbrushes, and give them to my team with instructions: I like the bristles on this one, the ferrule on that one, the handle on the other one. We created a line of fluffy brushes with real wood handles, the kind makeup artists would actually use, which I was proud of. On the side of the brushes we wrote what they were for—eyeliner, blush, and so on—instead of numbers, which was the norm and, in my opinion, confusing. The new creative environment allowed me to open up and share ideas that were so commonsense that they worked.

In the summer of 1996, Steven and I took the kids to Nantucket. Dylan and Cody began playing with an older girl on the beach. I struck up a conversation with her mother.

"What do you do?" I asked.

"I'm a book agent," she said.

"Oh, I'd love to write a book," I said. This wasn't some long-held dream. I liked books, but I had never really considered writing one before. On an instinctive level, I recognized an opportunity and responded to it. The woman asked about me, and I told her what I did for a living.

"I love your makeup and work!" she said. "I'd love to work on a book with you."

All of a sudden, I had a literary agent. Back in New York, I went to her office, where she explained the system: find a writer and write a proposal. I didn't know what I wanted to write about. One idea I had was to communicate my vision of beauty. I often felt frustrated with editorial photo shoots. On set I'd be blown away by how beautiful the models' faces looked, but often I'd open the magazine to find the editors had selected photos where the model's head was down, or an image with bad lighting. So I assembled every beautiful picture I had collected over the years and decided to put them in my book, which we called *Bobbi Brown Beauty*.

The book was more than just makeup tips. It reflected my beliefs on healthy eating, lifestyle, and exercise. Looking back I see I was making my version of the Cheryl Tiegs book I'd begged my dad to buy me as a teenager. But I filled my book with lessons I had learned in my thirty-nine years of searching.

As I worked on the book, I felt the interim corporate president at Bobbi Brown Cosmetics didn't see the bigger picture. "This has nothing to do with the company," I recall her saying. "We're not going to use company resources to promote it." To me, this didn't make sense. I knew from experience the more my name was out there, the better the sales for the brand. But when Maureen took over, she recognized the opportunities.

The book launched in 1997, a few months before my fortieth birthday. We threw a book party and invited the retailers, editors, models, and other important people in the business. Magazines covered the book or printed excerpts, good for both the book and the brand. My publisher landed me a spot on the *Today* show and scheduled a six-city book tour through Dallas, Los Angeles, Boston, Chicago, New York City, and Miami. Instead of holding events in bookstores, I scheduled appearances at Neiman Marcus stores in the area. I combined the book signing with makeup tutorials, which was also a great success for both book sales and our company. People would come in and get their makeup done, then buy a book and stand in line for a signature.

After a few of these events, I came up with a hack. It was exhausting to say to every woman, "What's your name, how do you spell it . . ." I couldn't keep the names straight. Instead, I'd have an assistant go down the aisle with a pack of sticky pads and a Sharpie, and while the women wrote their name and stuck it to the page where they wanted me to sign, the assistant would rub their hands with one of our creams. This helped make my job easier, kept the women busy while they were waiting, and promoted our product at the same time. After these events, I'd sit in my hotel room at night with the local account executive and sign hundreds of books. It was a fun, exciting time. How crazy that people wanted my signature on a book. My book.

So I was traveling again, packing my schedule with interviews, signings, and meetings. It's just what I did. I understood how important it was for the brand, although most of the time I would rather have been home in my kitchen, in big socks, making soup. Still, it's amazing how one opportunity led to another. At a book signing event in Miami, a sweet older lady raised her hand and said she'd seen me on the *Today* show promoting my book. "You've done so much. Is there anything else you want to do?"

"I'd like to be a regular on the *Today* show."

As it turned out, her grandson was Jeff Zucker, executive producer of the *Today* show. The book signing was on a Thursday; Jeff put me on the show the very next Monday. Thank you, Grandma Fran.

As I sat in the makeup chair before my first *Today* show appearance, my stomach churned with nerves. This was bigger than anything I had done before. Four and a half million people would be watching me. I wanted to seize the opportunity and educate women on how to do it all for themselves. I didn't want to be one of those flashy, campy makeup artists. I didn't want to hawk a product. In fact, in all my years on the show, I never talked about my makeup products. The anchors would say, "Next up, Bobbi Brown from Bobbi Brown Cosmetics." That was enough. I played the role of a beauty journalist. I wanted to give women practical advice. I might say, "If you're a working mom and you're late, you need these three things to get out the door in five minutes: a bone eye shadow, a taupe eye shadow, and a brown lipstick." Then I'd demonstrate. Or I'd say, "We did this on the runway at the Michael Kors show, but if you want to do it at home, here's how you should wear it." My audience was the women at home watching. These were the people I spoke to and developed products for.

After my first show, Jeff came to meet me. For some reason, he called me Barbara, and still does to this day. "Nice to meet you, Barbara," he said. "Grandma Fran said I should put you on the show."

"I love your grandma," I said. "She is so cute."

"What else do you want?" he asked.

I said the first thing that popped into my head: "Can I be a regular?"

"What do you mean?"

"Can I come on once a month?"

Jeff said yes, and the next month I was on the show again. He came down and said, "Barbara, that was great. Now what do you want?"

I noticed that everyone on the show had a title, so I said: "Can I have a title?"

"What title?"

"How about: 'Beauty editor of the *Today* show'?"

He said, "Hm, okay. You are the beauty editor." For the next fourteen years, I was introduced as "*Today* show Beauty Editor Bobbi Brown."

Talk about an explosion. Customers began running to the counter. The only thing more powerful than *Today* was when I'd appear on *Oprah*. That was a slam dunk. Every book became a bestseller. Every product I mentioned, gone. One time Oprah said, "I only wear Bobbi Brown foundation six, seven, and eight." After that, you could not buy foundation six, seven, and eight if your life depended on it. Even people with light skin were buying these dark browns. We had to instruct the shopgirls to explain to the customers how to buy the right color for their skin, rather than blindly following Oprah.

I'd become an internationally recognized beauty expert the same way I'd done everything in my career: by being myself and communicating my idea of beauty. I gave real advice, direct and simple. I created the looks on the runway, and then simplified those looks for real women. I taught working moms techniques to look good and make it simple and fast. My no-makeup makeup look, as well as my belief that we are all beautiful, no longer stood on the fringes of the industry. I had entered—and helped change—the mainstream. It is a true point of pride for me.

CHAPTER TWENTY-THREE

SOCCER MOM

Not everyone at Estée Lauder appreciated my approach. A top executive took me out to lunch and said, "I think you should buy a pied-à-terre in the city. You should show the beauty editors that you live this life. No one wants to take beauty advice from a soccer mom."

"But I am a soccer mom," I said.

Another executive, a very fancy, beloved woman who had been around forever, said to me, "Darling, you're very demure and very petite. I think you need a signature so when you walk in a room people notice you. I suggest wearing a hat with a feather."

Then there was the hairdresser who told me I needed to cut my hair and adopt a style, or I wouldn't work in the industry. I tried— but went right back to my old style. And there was the former beauty editor we hired who took me shopping in SoHo and pressured me into buying leather pants and other outfits that were so not me. "They look amazing," she said. "You just gotta get used to it." I never wore them because they looked terrible on me and I didn't feel right.

I guess I could have transformed myself into a fabulous New York character—so many of my peers were cool and larger than life. And sometimes they're the most interesting people. But that's not me. I absorbed the experiences I had with these people, but then I'd head home to my husband and put dinner on the table for my children. I chose that because I felt the most comfortable being myself.

By being myself, and remaining true to my philosophy and my identity, I was starting to create a culture around the brand. Whatever I was into at the time became part of that culture. At meetings, we didn't serve bagels, cookies, or Danishes, because I was into healthy eating, and I saw how everyone would crash after eating that way. Instead, we'd serve almonds, yogurt, granola, and dark chocolate. Corporate executives would come in looking for a sandwich platter and cookies and they'd find grilled chicken, salmon, greens, and quinoa. They'd open the fridge looking for a soda and find fresh juice and sparkling water.

At sales meetings, we'd blast Mary J. Blige and create playlists that worked with the direction of the season. We also created guidebooks of how best to represent the brand: what to serve at press events, what kind of music to play, how the waiters should be dressed. The result was a booming business and a company and culture that made me proud.

In 1998, baby Duke joined his brothers—six-year-old Dakota and eight-year-old Dylan. Duke was a happy, easy creature, a little sponge absorbing all the busy and doting people around him—our nuclear family and also nieces, nephews, and friends. Now, in addition to my work bags, I carried a bag full of spare diapers, burp cloths, formula, and baby clothes. At forty-one years old, I had three boys who fought as hard as they played, a successful makeup company, a monthly gig on the *Today* show, and a new career as an author. My life was fuller than ever, and I loved it.

I poured the same creativity into developing new products at work that I poured into, say, planning a birthday party. For one of Duke's, everyone brought their plastic riding cars and we made a little drive-in window with hot dogs. The day of the party, when I went to buy balloons, I saw a parking meter maid in Montclair (her name was Rita, funnily enough) and I paid her to come write the kids traffic tickets as they "drove" across the lawn.

I volunteered every year to be a class mom, which was more stressful than live TV. But I wanted to be the mom who came in on Fridays and read books to the class. Where did I find the time? I have no idea. One of my jobs was to organize the kindergarten class trips. The teacher wanted one trip a month for the whole school year. On one trip, we took the kids to a construction project Steven was working on to show them big trucks and equipment. Another time we went to the supermarket and talked to the grocers about their jobs.

It didn't always go smoothly. When Duke was in kindergarten,

I was supposed to buy googly eyes for a project. I had a very long day at work, and in the car coming home, I realized, *Oh my God, I forgot to buy the googly eyes.* I didn't worry about much, but I definitely worried about disappointing my kids. I called Steven, begging for help. No bite there. So I said to the driver, "Please, let's go to Staples," hoping we'd arrive before the store closed. We did, but they were out of googly eyes. Same with Kmart next door, and there was no time to get to the art store in the next town. Okay, now what? I picked up my phone and sent an email to my friends in Montclair: "Help! 911! Does anyone have any googly eyes?" People started dropping off googly eyes at my house. By about ten thirty that night, I had a shoebox full of them. I was proud of myself that I solved this problem. The next day, I asked Duke, "How did the googly eyes project go?"

"The teacher was sick," he said. "We didn't do it."

Oh well.

I tried hard to be present for my kids. I certainly wasn't perfect. Cody reminds me that once or twice I forgot to pick him up at school. In pre-K, Duke had blocks fall on his head and Steven had to take him to the emergency room because I was working. I felt terrible about these things. But I attended almost every school sing-along. As the kids got older, between the soccer games, after-school events, and homework, I really had to push myself to keep up, but I did it because I loved being part of a community, sharing this camaraderie with the teachers and parents, and I absolutely loved raising my kids.

By 2004, when my kids were all in school, I started spending less time in the office, occasionally working from home. This actually helped me. In the office, I was tied up in meetings. At home, I could process the happenings of the day, then actually sit down and do some work or make phone calls uninterrupted, while taking short breaks to prepare dinner or tidy the house. I wanted the incredible life experiences that my job afforded, but I also wanted a flourishing home life too. I was lucky to experience both.

CHAPTER TWENTY-FOUR

BE NORMAL

I've always felt best when I can just be me. Wherever I go, and whoever I'm with, whether presidents, dignitaries, or celebrities, I'm still Bobbi. It comes from my upbringing—from Nana and Papa Sam, from my parents, from Aunt Alice, and of course from Steven—and it also comes from the choices I have made, and the experiences I've had.

I've seen my share of divas and prima donnas, and I decided I never wanted to be like them. I've also seen the opposite: people at the top of their field who remain nice, normal, down-to-earth, and kind. I'll never forget watching Cindy Crawford get a terrible blowout and saying to the hairdresser, "Thank you so much, I really appreciate it." After the hairdresser left, she grabbed a brush and fixed her hair.

I remember doing Diane Sawyer's makeup and handing her a mirror to check it. "I'm sure it's fine," she said, waving the mirror away.

Then there was Meryl Streep, who arrived at the shoot by herself—no handlers, no agent, no entourage.

On one job, I struggled to do Susan Sarandon's makeup because she wouldn't look at me. Instead, she was looking down, answering letters from women in prison. I ended up working with Susan often, and she became a role model for me. She advised me to hire a housekeeper on Saturdays so I could be free to just play with my kids. Instead, I hired a babysitter to take the kids to the park so I could clean and organize my house.

To witness and be around heroes in my life, like Yogi Berra or Neil Armstrong or Gloria Steinem, who each share a common attribute of down-to-earth kindness, made a giant impact on me. I've chosen to surround myself with normal people. To me, being normal has nothing to do with one's status, income, or title. To me, being normal means treating people with decency and respect. It means valuing family and relationships over business and profit. It means remaining true to yourself and where you come from, no matter where you go.

I had tea once with Princess Eugenie, granddaughter of Queen Elizabeth II, and I asked about their relationship. She said, "When Grandma is in the palace, it's more formal, and I schedule an appointment and always dress up, but when we're in our country house, we just wear our pajamas and watch the telly." And I thought, *Of course you do.* She might be Queen Elizabeth, but when you're across from her at the breakfast table in the country house, she's just Grandma.

Normal.

One of my proudest achievements came when I was touring the Bobbi Brown Cosmetics stores in Asia and having my makeup artists tell me they never knew it was possible to work and have a family until they started working for me. One employee in China made a beautiful video of her day: getting up in the morning, taking care of her child, going to work at the makeup counter, coming home and making dinner for her family.

She'd watched me do it and knew she could do it too. In Korea and Japan, the women I encountered said they had always been told their skin was the wrong color. No one ever told them they were beautiful. I came with a different message. I think Asian women are some of the most beautiful women in the world. My makeup, my brand, my aesthetic gave these women a new way to see themselves. That's the power of being normal. It doesn't matter whether you're a successful businesswoman, a famous actor, or a shopgirl in Asia. Normal is beautiful.

BOBBI BROWN essentials

PART SIX

SHIT
HAPPENS

CHAPTER TWENTY-FIVE

MOTHER OF INVENTION

My best ideas come when I don't look for them. In the early 2000s, *Architectural Digest* came to our home in Telluride, Colorado, for an article and photo shoot, after which they needed to reshoot a few photos, so I had them send the photographer over by himself, rather than get the whole production involved. As I did my makeup, I realized I had forgotten my makeup bag at home in Montclair. After doing the best I could with a black mascara and no eye shadow, I noticed something was missing. I needed to line my top eye to look awake. I thought and acted fast. I took the fuzzy end off a Q-tip, dipped it in my mascara, and lined my eyes with it. I had also forgotten my makeup remover, so that night I went to bed with the makeshift eyeliner still on. The next morning, I woke up, looked in the mirror, and realized my mistake. I called Gabrielle, my head of product development. "Gab," I said, "call the lab and ask them if it's okay." A few minutes later, Gab called back. "They said it's fine because it's gel based," she said. I don't know why that made it okay. I just accepted it.

That gave me a vision.

I used to go to vintage stores and buy cool stuff for my desk, and one of my favorite pieces was this funky old inkwell. "Gab," I said, "you know that little vintage ink bottle I have on my desk? What if we made the packaging look like that, pour the mascara formula into it, and call it 'gel ink'?" And that's just what we did. I had accidentally created not just a new product but a whole new category: gel ink. A decade later, it was our number-one-selling product. Every other cosmetic brand also began to make its own version, as does Jones Road.

While my creative team understood my vision, I often got push-back from those in corporate who didn't. When I wanted to make a foundation stick, they said, "No one wants a foundation stick." They could only imagine that super-dry, cakey stick that was part of stage makeup. I had in mind something else, something much more wearable and modern, something light and portable that women could use in the back of a cab or on the way to drop the kids at school. The idea was based on my lifestyle and the women I knew. Not only did the Bobbi Brown Foundation Stick become wildly successful, it also changed the market.

Then there was pot rouge: creamy blush in a pot that women could apply with their fingers. I came up with the idea reminiscing about the way Nana used to put on her lipstick, tap it with her fingers, and rub it on her cheeks. As a makeup artist, I often found myself using lipstick as a blush in a similar way. People said, "No one wants to use their fingers for application." I didn't listen. Pot Rouge became another huge seller.

Not every idea was mine. One of our best inventions, the Shimmer Brick, came from the lab. I thought it looked gimmicky, but someone said, "Just try it." I put a brush in it and applied it to my face, and Wow! Again, there was nothing like it on the market. It became another huge hit.

Around this time, I noticed that when we'd go to Telluride, a town with a very high altitude, my skin would get really dry and I couldn't find a moisturizer that worked. We came up with a dense cream for really dry skin. I loved the product, but no one could think of a name. We had all these consultants and executives pitching ideas, but nothing stuck. I was complaining to Steven in the car one day with the kids in the back, when eight-year-old Cody piped up: "Why don't you just call it Extra?" Done. Another hit.

Cody wasn't the only family member getting in on the action. Aunt Alice could never find lipstick she liked, so I brought her into the lab and we worked together to make the color of her dreams, pale pink with blue undertones. The team said it wouldn't sell. Pale Mauve, as we called it, ended up being the best-selling color in Asia.

Not every idea worked. In the mid-2000s, the department store was all flash and glam. Bobbi Brown Cosmetics, with our subdued tones and packaging, looked a little flat. We panicked and created a subline called Color Options. Our concept: when a woman wears a little black dress, she needs rhinestone earrings or a bold color pop to dress it up. Why can't we do that with makeup? Why can't we create these fun, shimmery, bold colors women can use when they want to take it up a notch? We designed cool packaging, bold and bright colors, dense textures, and lots of glitter. At first it boosted sales. But the makeup artists got overexcited and started applying it all at once. Women walked away from the counter looking like they just had a bad department-store makeover. It didn't work. Plus, it took away from the essence of the brand.

We quickly went back to what we were known for and what I believed in, focusing on nudes and what that meant for all skin tones. Nudes to me have always been to match colors to what is naturally visible on the skin. Nudes were a big hit and reinforced what the makeup brand was about.

I love creating. I think about new products and I think about the way they'd fit a theme, the same way a fashion designer thinks about their collections all the time. Whether the season was about nudes, pinks, browns, or chocolates, it was always so much fun coming up with how we were going to bring it to life, from what the name was, to how to photograph it, to how it looked in bags at events, at sales meetings, and in stores. I loved the camaraderie with the teams and everyone throwing out ideas to achieve our goal.

Once the collection was approved, we next had to inspire our team. We'd have our global makeup artists come to New York for training and a collection-themed party. Then they'd have operational meetings to discuss logistics. At night we'd have a big, themed party. Then they'd go back home and start their work, bringing the new collection to their team and the customers, while I moved on to the next season.

Working at Estée Lauder was like getting a business degree. I learned the business of anniversarying: if we had a blowout success, we had to do something just as big, if not bigger, at the same time the next year. Once we launched a new formula of lipsticks, our CFO David Nass, who always took time to explain the finances to me, came into my office with a sales report. The new lipstick was selling well, which I thought was a reason to celebrate, but David did not look happy. "The new lipstick formula is cannibalizing our normal, day-to-day business," he said. I didn't know what "cannibalization" meant. "Let me explain," he said. "We sold a few million units of the new lipstick, but our basic lipstick business stalled. People are buying the new, not the classics."

He said because we forecasted the classics to be higher, we were $3 million behind our projections. David explained that the whole launch took all the resources to promote and left us short. We needed to make up the difference. But how? He explained that some star products do a million dollars per color, such as bronzers.

"No problem," I said. "I have two or three colors of bronzer in my head." We brought out three new bronzers and made the season. We named one Elvis Duran, after the radio personality, who is also a good friend.

I loved the challenge and learned a lot. When provided with information and facts, I instantly put both sides of my brain to use and loved the challenge of figuring out what to do. But, on occasion, I went against the information and fought hard for what I believed in. For example, I was asked to discontinue the darkest shades that weren't selling well, but I refused. It was important to me that whoever came to the counter would find a color that worked for them, no matter their skin tone, whether in a blush, a foundation, or a lipstick. Being inclusive has become a trend, but it was always common sense to me. It took a lot of maneuvering and negotiating, but that was a fight I wasn't going to lose.

To me, being inclusive went beyond skin color. I've always championed age as a positive thing. In 2007, I turned fifty and released my fourth book, *Living Beauty*, teaching women of a certain age how to use makeup rather than surgery to enhance their beauty. I wanted to change the conversation around aging to positive living. There was so much pressure on women to look younger. I said, "Let's drop the word 'younger' and focus on 'fresher' or 'healthier.'"

Turning fifty was a huge milestone, especially as a woman in the beauty business. But I didn't see aging as an obstacle, and I still don't. As I got older, I became more comfortable and confident. I started to listen and pay attention to how I felt. I mastered using makeup to not look tired, but then I also began seeking out wellness practices to not feel tired. To support my health, under holistic doctors, I began using bioidentical hormones and adapting my diet and lifestyle to feel better. I made sure to eat food to fuel my body every day—more veggies, protein, fiber, and the right fat. It made me feel better. I'd limit the foods that didn't make me feel good until I didn't crave them any longer—like cookies and pastries. I started paying attention to my sleep and seeing holistic health practitioners who helped support and educate me. It became yet another passion and part of my curiosity.

Even though I felt good, and the number fifty didn't bother

me, there were a lot of changes that year. It was Dylan's last year of high school, the last year of my family as I knew it. I think most parents of college-age kids know that bittersweet mixture of pride and heartbreak. Dylan got into Stanford, which made me so proud. I thought back to myself enrolling at Arizona because it was the only school I could get in to, and wondered how I had created this brilliant kid. At the same time, I knew that once he left, nothing would be the same.

We decided to throw Dylan a graduation party in our backyard, and I went to Costco to buy supplies. I'll never forget walking down one of the aisles and seeing diapers, baby wipes, and Tampax. And then Depends! It felt like Costco was giving me some sort of cosmic message. I stood there, choked up, thinking: *I'm done with diapers; I'm done with wipes; I'm done with Tampax.* Then I saw the next item on the shelf: Depend adult diapers.

Nope. Not there yet!

CHAPTER TWENTY-SIX

MAKEUP ARTIST IN CHIEF

My life, which had already been full of incredible "pinch me" moments, had become more surreal than ever. A few days before my fiftieth birthday, the *Today* show did a segment to celebrate this milestone, and I talked about my Ali MacGraw *Love Story* revelation. On my actual birthday, I was at home, when my phone rang.

"Bobbi?" said an unfamiliar voice.

"Yes?"

"This is Ali."

"Ali who?"

"Ali MacGraw."

"Yeah, right."

"No, really. I saw you yesterday on the *Today* show, and I was so honored. I've been wearing your makeup since it came out. I'm such a fan."

Pinch me.

I ended up meeting Ali in London for tea the following year. Talk about an out-of-body experience. I don't even remember much of what happened except that she talked really fast and we discussed working together, but it hasn't happened . . . yet.

Another call on my birthday came from a young senator and fellow Chicago native named Barack Obama. A few years prior, Steven and I held a fundraiser at our house for a candidate running for senator of New Jersey, and Barack came to our house to show support. When he walked in the house, a line of people formed waiting to greet him, to speak with him, to shake his hand. I noticed him trapped in this whirlwind, caught his eye, and mouthed, "Do you have to use the bathroom?" He nodded. I took him upstairs to the boys' bathroom. He came out and said, "It's so nice to meet you. Michelle is a big fan."

He was awesome and so real. We connected. When he called me at work to wish me a happy fiftieth birthday, I asked if he was running for president. He told me he'd let us know. A bit after, he called Steven and told him he was going to run, and asked us for our support. When he won, I was hired to do Jill Biden's makeup for the inauguration ceremony. It was surreal.

I had been to many famous, cool, incredible places with many famous, cool, and incredible people, but now I was a witness to history. While I was riding in the presidential motorcade en route to the inauguration, a man in the car turned to me and said, "Who are you?" I told him I was Jill's makeup artist and asked him who he was. "I'm Leon Panetta," he said, "your secretary of defense." I asked to have a photo. When we finally arrived at the White House, I followed Jill and Michelle with my little makeup bag as they went backstage. As I stood at the end of the line with Dr. Biden's chief of staff, waiting for them to get inaugurated, I took a candid picture of Barack's special assistant Reggie Love handing his boss a water bottle before Obama walked out to become the next president. It was so magical to witness history. Then I was moved into a side room to do touch-ups as needed. In walked Joe Biden. I said, "I'm not sure what to call you." What do you say to the man who has just taken the oath as vice president of the United States? He said, "Bobbi, just call me Joe."

After that, Steven and I were often invited to Christmas and Hanukkah parties and other events at the White House. Those were always so interesting. The line for the coat check at the White House was a who's who of actors, designers, politicians, businesspeople, musicians, and dignitaries, all of us awed by the experience.

Sometimes when Steven didn't make the trip, I'd take one of the kids or my dad. One year, I took my dad to the Hanukkah party and at the buffet I found myself next to Ruth Bader Ginsburg putting latkes on her plate. My dad snapped a picture.

As always, my family shared in my milestones. My dad came to many celebrations, whether it was a book party or a product launch.

When he started writing children's books, my PR team created a book tour for him and me. My mom was equally proud. She wanted me to open a store in her retirement community.

Steven's parents, whom I adored, were there too. My father-in-law, Mort, always wore Bobbi Brown sweatshirts and hats. He'd come over with his tools and fix whatever had to be fixed. One day I borrowed his tool belt to use it as a template to make a brush belt for my artists. Steven's mother, Ev (short for Evelyn), was a very simple woman. I did a before-and-after on her for one of my books, and I heard from Mort that it was the most amazing thing she had ever experienced. She had this friend who was always bragging about her daughter. One day the lady said, "My daughter just got the best job. She works at Saks for a makeup company."

"What company?" Ev asked.

"You wouldn't know it," the woman answered.

Ev said, "Try me."

"It's called Bobbi Brown."

"That's my daughter-in-law." Game, set, match, Ev.

Throughout my life and career, I have always seemed to find my people, the real people who share my dedication to family. That's what I found in the Obamas. Soon Michelle began inviting me to accompany her in her work with high school girls at the White House. At these events, I'd speak to these kids alongside the White House chef and trainer on health and wellness. I brought retouched beauty photos and showed the girls how unrealistic they were. I wanted to share what the beauty industry is really like. I had written two books for teenagers and gave everyone a book. Then I'd go back to the White House for a dinner where Sheryl Crow or Alicia Keys would perform while I sat at a table packed with interesting people. One time it was Viola Davis; Reese Witherspoon; Michelle's mother, Marian; and me, pinching myself once again.

In the middle of 2010, my assistant came into my office and said, "The president is on the phone and would like to talk to you." I knew it wasn't a joke. I picked up the phone.

"Hi, Bobbi," Barack said. "I'd like to appoint you to the Advisory Committee for Trade Policy and Negotiations."

I was flabbergasted, but before answering I called Steven to get his opinion.

"You hate committees," he said. "You're going to be bored."

True. But then again, this was a committee I couldn't refuse. How few people even get to go to the White House, let alone regularly? If nothing else, I knew it was an opportunity that might never come again.

First, I had to get confirmed. Canvassers went neighbor to neighbor, knocked on every door, and asked about me. They found people who knew me in kindergarten. The FBI showed up unannounced to my office one day, their guns at their hips. Maureen came in and said, "What are you guys, male strippers?"

Once confirmed, I had to attend one meeting per month. It wasn't just showing up at a meeting, though. I had to pack a bag, get on a plane or a train, arrive the night before, sleep in a hotel—the whole production of traveling—all for a one-hour meeting. Then I'd head home again.

The meetings were just what you think when you hear the word "committee": roll call, then someone would read the minutes, then we'd talk about the different laws that had to be passed and the challenges facing American business around the world. Then we went around the room, which was full of an unusual array of people such as New Jersey Governor Chris Christie; the mayor of Orlando, Florida; Jimmy Hoffa's son; and the head of the pork belly coalition, and everyone was allowed to say one thing. When it got to me, I'd always say, "Have you ever thought about this . . ." I'm a problem solver, though I'm not sure anyone ever acted on my advice. On one occasion, Barack walked in and said, "Nice kicks, B Squared," and I looked up and thought of how proud Papa Sam would have been of me.

I stayed on the trade commission for one term, but I did makeup for two inaugurations. I got to know the Bidens. They called me Bobbi Biden. They were as kind to Steven as they were to me. They made these experiences so much better. It's cool to meet famous people, but what I really love is when you cut through the bullshit and see the real person behind the persona.

CHAPTER TWENTY-SEVEN

THE BEST OF TIMES

In 2011, we celebrated twenty years of Bobbi Brown Cosmetics with a collection called Party, including a perfume called Bobbi's Party, based on the fragrance Aunt Alice always wore. We also made a new lipstick called Party Alice that I envisioned her wearing if she went to a fancy party. We hosted lavish parties at the ambassador's residences in Paris, London, and Beijing. We hired Bruce Weber to make a film, *The Wise-Cracking Beauty Queen*, which was, as he described it, a love letter to me. It was an incredible celebration and a highlight of my career. That same year, Kate Middleton wore Bobbi Brown Cosmetics on her wedding day, and one of my makeup artists in England did her makeup. I was obsessed with the royal family, so this was a huge honor, as well as evidence that my concept of beauty had impacted the world. It was hard to believe how far makeup had taken me.

I still saw myself as a makeup artist before anything. Around this time I was asked to key a fashion show in London for the fashion designer L'Wren Scott. I went there for the makeup test and we stayed for hours trying different looks. Later, L'Wren's boyfriend— Mick Jagger—arrived to check our progress and offer his opinion. It's cool to say I collaborated on a makeup test with Sir Mick! After the test, his chef brought us dinner. As we ate the most delicious Moroccan food, I told him about the time I was a young makeup artist and I did his makeup for an Annie Leibovitz shoot. He couldn't have been nicer.

Mick wasn't the only rock 'n' roll royalty in my orbit. I also met and became close with Bruce Springsteen's wife, Patti Scialfa. When Bruce put together the 12-12-12 concert for Hurricane Sandy relief, I was asked to do their makeup for the show. Twenty-plus years before that night, I'd slept at a New Jersey mall to get tickets to see Bruce. Now I was in his house doing his makeup. Bruce was a god and yet still real. When it came time to drive to Madison Square Garden, they had two cars: one for the hair, makeup, and stylists, and one for Bruce and his family. As I was about to get in the other car, Patti called to me and said, "Bobbi, come with us." Off I went in a car with the Boss and his wife, discussing the adrenaline of performing and what we liked to eat afterward. He was performing for tens of thousands of screaming fans, and I was performing on

QVC, but Bruce and I ate the same snack: Ezekiel bread, organic peanut butter, and jam. I had brought my old 8-track of one of Bruce's albums and asked him to sign it. Then the phone rang, and I heard Bruce say, "Bobby, how ya doin'?" It was Bob Dylan. As someone who named her first kid Dylan, you can imagine how I felt. The concert was a who's who of music royalty, everyone from Billy Joel and the Rolling Stones to Bon Jovi and Paul McCartney. At one point, Sting's wife, Trudie, came into the dressing room to hang out, and I ended up doing downward-facing dog yoga poses with her. These moments felt like dreams.

Then came the Met Gala. The Met Gala is like the Super Bowl of fashion. The who's who of fashion, business, music, and celebrity all jockey to attend. I had done makeup for celebrities before, but now I was invited as a guest, which happens only if Anna Wintour approves. When the invitation arrived, I was psyched, followed by, *Oh shit, what am I going to wear?* The angst and anxiety set in. Most people have their agents call their beauty team and stylist and designers. I didn't have stylists. I was always on the beauty team. Now I needed them.

Thankfully, Steven was also invited. We pulled up in a limo to the New York Metropolitan Museum of Art and waited in line for our turn on the red carpet. The more famous you are, the later you go. Needless to say, we went pretty early.

Then comes the big moment: strolling down the red carpet. The flashbulbs are popping and the crowds on the street are all screaming. It's pure madness. I felt like a pinball in a machine. And then all of a sudden, I'm standing amid a sea of celebrities, designers, actors, artists, and musicians.

After the red carpet, we stood in line to say hello to Anna, the chairperson of the Met Gala, and the other hosts. I had done Anna's makeup a few times, so we knew each other. Steven wore his new tux. I had decided on a cute Prada skirt suit with super-high, off-white shoes, until I fell off a curb and broke my foot. Instead of heels, I wore white Jack Purcell sneakers. As Anna greeted me, her eyes scanned down my body and stopped at my sneakers.

"I broke my foot," I explained.

"I didn't think it was a fashion statement," she said, and walked away with her head cocked in that inimitable way.

Inside the museum, waiters served hors d'oeuvres while the guests milled around enjoying the fashion exhibits. I headed straight for the bar to collect myself. Then I went to the bathroom and stood at a sink next to Amal Alamuddin, the future Mrs. Clooney, while famous actresses and models touched up their makeup nearby.

At another Met Gala, I did Rosario Dawson's makeup, in addition to attending myself. I had to get her ready, then run to get dressed for my appearance. That year I wore a beautiful navy silk tuxedo from Sandro and the highest red heels I'd ever seen. I thought I looked amazing. No one probably noticed me with Rihanna standing there in Christian Louboutin shoes, Cartier jewels, and a nearly see-through white Stella McCartney gown, while next to her were Tom Brady and Gisele, Kim Kardashian and Kanye, and Beyoncé and Jay-Z, and they weren't just wearing beautiful clothes, they were all trying to make a statement.

I finally walked the red carpet behind Kerry Washington and her husband. I knew her a little bit. We looked at each other like, *Oh shit, here goes.* Then she stepped out and the paparazzi bulbs burst, and I followed tottering in those uncomfortable shoes.

I loved these events, and I was honored to be invited, but after the second one, I was done. The further I got into my fifties, the more comfortable I became saying no. I don't want to go somewhere and be fabulous. I don't want to put on a gown and high heels and spend all night in New York City at an event outside my comfort zone. I'd rather go somewhere where I can dress in comfortable clothes with messy hair and still feel fabulous because the people there love me and are happy to see me. It took time to get to that point.

To support a few philanthropic endeavors, I joined the board of Citymeals on Wheels, which fed homebound elderly people. It's an incredible organization that the board at Lauder also supported. I joined the board of Dress For Success, a nonprofit helping unemployed women achieve economic independence by providing support, professional attire, and training on how to thrive in the job market. One year, I put together a fundraiser with photographers, hairstylists, and makeup artists who donated their time to give our clients the full *Vogue* experience. We supplied makeup kits for all clients of the American DFS so they'd feel beautiful and confident and ready to enter the workforce.

With support from Maureen, we adopted a high school in the Bronx called Jane Addams, which had a cosmetology program for kids in need and a nursery for the students who had kids. I first visited the school through New York City's Principal For A Day program, and I fell in love with it. I'd go there and teach different subjects related to makeup and think of other unique ways to support the school. For years we had spent a lot of money on Hermès or Loro

Piano scarves or socks as gifts to editors and tastemakers. I realized we could do so much good with those resources, so we created a four-year college scholarship. Applicants wrote an essay about how college would change their life. The next year, we refurbished the school nursery with help from Pottery Barn Kids, and then we made over the cosmetology classroom.

I read a story about a woman named Liz Murray in *The New York Times* and asked her to be photographed for one of my books. I mentioned Liz Murray earlier—she is the author of one of my favorite books, *Breaking Night*, and originator of the phrase "So what, now what?" which I'd had blown up and painted on my office wall. After she graduated from Harvard, Liz began working with the Broome Street Academy, a high school in SoHo that helps students in need. She brought me in to see the school and speak, and I instantly wanted to be part of it. We began offering support and resources. A lot of these kids didn't even have a bed to call their own, so they certainly didn't have pencils and notebooks. Then we sent several of our team members to the school to speak to the students about different careers like PR and communications, logistics, etc. We wanted them to know that opportunities are everywhere, and we wanted to provide those opportunities whenever we could.

Pinch me. We were empowering women not just with makeup but also with opportunity. We were giving back to the world. Best of all, the success of Bobbi Brown Cosmetics meant my philosophy on beauty and wellness helped shift the conversation to define beauty as more than just how you look or what you put on your skin. I had an incredible team around me, including Maureen (president), Veronika (head of global communications), Gabrielle (head of product development), David (CFO), and dozens of other people at all levels of the business all over the world. They stoked my enthusiasm and helped bring my ideas to life, but also felt free to tell me the idea wouldn't work. I don't like yes people—but, rather, people who are able to be truthful and direct without being intimidated. We had a common goal: to win.

The beliefs I had through the years—that real faces are beautiful; that makeup should enhance, not cover up; that feeling good is as important as looking good—these became the DNA of the brand. We were becoming bigger than makeup. We had a unique office with yoga, a manicurist, dogs, and guest speakers on business, investing, health, and wellness. This was our Camelot.

EST.
1991

CHAPTER TWENTY-EIGHT

THE WORST
OF TIMES

Everything was great . . . until it wasn't. It took me a while to notice things were changing. My beloved magazines were struggling
to survive. The editors, photographers, and magazines I loved were
being elbowed out by Instagram influencers and YouTube tutorials.
These changes I could live with. I had spent my life adapting.

I had a more difficult time with changes internally. In 2009, the
corp. hired a new CEO with a different style than his predecessors.
Things changed slowly at first, but by the time I released my book
Pretty Powerful in 2012, I definitely felt something wasn't right. The

book was an encouragement for women to start with who you are and just be you as your best self. I interviewed dozens of real women, celebrities, and athletes about what beauty means to them, and then showed, step by step, how to achieve certain looks. In my mind, the book was a launching pad for the next global brand initiative, centered on this phrase to remind women that they could be pretty and powerful, that pretty is powerful, and that we are all pretty powerful. We ran into trouble with some global markets because "pretty powerful" is an American expression, so when they translated it, it didn't have the same meaning. I argued to keep Pretty Powerful in English all over the world, and just educate our global teams about what it meant. I saw it as a slogan, like Nike's Just Do It. But the company had hired a slew of new people in the foreign markets. They did not understand my vision, and no one on my team could convince them. They insisted on translating Pretty Powerful into different languages. The messaging got completely scrambled.

The head office didn't seem to understand my vision. At one of our meetings, as I recall it, the new CEO declared: "Women don't want to be pretty. Pretty is for girls. A woman wants to be beautiful."

I begged to differ and said so.

My team couldn't believe I had just challenged the CEO. He had put together a team, mostly men, who would never openly disagree with him in a meeting.

I used to look forward to these meetings. They were interesting and invigorating. I loved talking to the team, bouncing ideas back and forth, and working together to perfect our global messaging and marketing. But as the meetings got bigger and bigger, they became more formal and less invigorating for me.

The optimism was replaced with stress and fear. My team would endeavor for six months to prepare our presentations. Then we'd trudge up to the forty-second floor of the GM Building to find forty people sitting around a huge oval table with little microphones like at the UN. You had to press a red button to speak. Above our heads hung screens with associates conferencing from all around the world. Corporate employees sat on one side of the table and the brand team sat on the other side.

I never felt intimidated. I knew how to make and market makeup. I understood what women wanted, no matter where they came from. I wanted the brand I created to talk to people the way I would talk to people—truthfully and directly. I had an ideal customer in mind. I called her Mrs. Schwartz. Whenever we created something new, I'd ask my team, "When Mrs. Schwartz comes to the counter, will she understand this?"

But under these circumstances, my team struggled. I blame myself. I wanted Maureen to be paid more, and corporate said the only way to do that was to put her in charge of more brands. When this happened, I should have insisted on a structure that gave both her and us more support.

Maureen had a difficult time. She believed in our brand, but the stress and her bosses were pulling her apart. Veronika, our head of global communications, struggled too. She knew me well and understood what I wanted and didn't want, but she had two corporate leaders and three brand presidents telling her what to do.

Things were starting to unravel, and I was frustrated and aggravated. We had thirty freestanding stores, along with a presence in one thousand other doors, spread across sixty countries. Add in new people in finance and wholesale, plus all the international regions that reported to regional heads, and it got too big and too complicated. It wasn't relying on the strengths of a founder anymore and the original vision; it was built to homogenize all the brands. And I didn't have Leonard in my corner saying, "Yes, Bobbi," anymore; corporate powers had apparently shifted.

Leonard had been a brand builder. The new executives saw the numbers and trends pointing in a direction and wanted every brand to go in that direction. Instead of letting Bobbi Brown do what we did best, they tried to push us into whatever looked profitable and competitive at the moment.

At one meeting, I felt pressured to create a skin whitener because that was the top-selling product in Asia. But I had spent twenty years urging people to choose a foundation that matched their skin and not use makeup to lighten it. How would it look if I suddenly came out with a skin whitener?

"You don't understand," I was told. "This is a big category, and if we don't make it, we're not going to be competitive in Asia."

I consider myself a reasonable person. I like to hear other people's ideas. But I'm a fighter when I believe in something.

"Explain why people want whitening cream," I said.

"They want to have a brighter complexion."

"Then why don't we make a brightening cream?" I said.

We compromised. We didn't tell people their skin should be whiter, just that it could be brighter. I refused to market it as changing the color of your skin. It ended up being a fun challenge for me, but I'm sure the people at the top felt frustrated.

Another time one of the corporate guys showed me this thick

concealer that was so not a Bobbi Brown product. I hated it. I said no way.

"Bobbi," he said, "if you don't approve this immediately, we'll miss projections for the season."

"Fine," I said. "Miss it."

It somehow got added to the launch calendar without my approval and was released anyway.

Perhaps the biggest fight came over contouring, which was having a resurgence among social-media influencers. At the time, everyone wanted to look like a doll, using the darkest foundation stick available to contour their face into oblivion. Corporate wanted me to cash in on the trend, but I refused. I just couldn't do it. I never liked contouring. To me, it looks fake, and I don't like fake. I was always teaching women they are beautiful as they are. They kept insisting. I kept refusing. The fight reached a ridiculous point when corporate suggested that I appear at Beautycon, a gathering of all the influencers and social media junkies who were into heavy makeup, baking, contouring—everything we weren't. The PR team knew I'd hate it there, so they came to me with a compromise: What if we made a hologram of me, like they did with Tupac? Beautycon was so into the idea they offered to give us the main stage for free. That was the stupidest idea I had ever heard. It wasn't me, it wasn't authentic, and I refused to do it.

Meanwhile, Veronika would catch hell when I posted something on the brand's Instagram. The higher-ups would demand: "Why is she posting pictures of her dogs or the salad she's eating?" They wanted three posts on the next lipstick, and a contouring palette, and user-generated content from influencers, with everything planned out a month in advance. That's not what I wanted and not what I believed in.

The more I said no to these terrible ideas, the more I noticed things happening without my consent. Around this time, I left a photo shoot and the creative director decided to style a wildly retouched, white, pasty model wearing a black leather glove and dark purple lipstick, grimacing into the camera. It didn't look like beautiful skin and happy models. It looked like Elvira wearing bad makeup. Thankfully, the global teams hated it and I was able to stop it from seeing print.

I began to dread going to work. Most days I came home angry and vented to Steven. "Why don't you just leave?" he asked. But I couldn't. This was my company. It had my name, my face, and my philosophy attached to it. It was the number one artist-created brand in the world, selling 220 million products per year. I kept thinking I could fix it. If I could just find the right people and say the right thing. If, if, if. I got through a week thinking it was going to get better. A week turned into a month, a month turned into a year, then two, then three, and I woke up one day and thought, *What the hell happened?*

Bobbi believes that skin should look like skin. Your radiance should shine through.

CHAPTER TWENTY-NINE

FAMOUS
LAST
WORDS

Everything was crumbling. We had no leadership and no consistency. I'd look at my team and see that they didn't know what to do anymore. Many of them quit and were replaced with corporate types who didn't fit our vibe or understand our point of view. I'll never forget the ad campaign where we chose a model with a gap in her teeth only to find that in some regions they retouched the photo to fill in the gap. I was furious, and I only became more so as decisions at the brand kept getting made without me.

One day, a global sales executive came in and pitched me an idea that I rejected as totally off-brand. Or at least I thought she was pitching me. As it turned out, she had already implemented it without my consent.

This painful disconnection at work was mirrored by a challenging time at home. Dylan and Cody had left for college, and Duke was about to spend his sophomore year of high school out of state. I remember coming home one day, stressed and overwhelmed. For the first time in a long time, I didn't trip over a pile of shoes. Then it hit me: no shoes meant no boys. I was suddenly an empty nester, and didn't have my home life to distract me from my troubles at work. My house was finally clean, but I felt sad. I was so happy at Thanksgiving when the kids and their friends returned and messed up my hallway with a pile of beautiful shoes and sneakers. They looked like gold to me.

Still, I didn't realize I was losing my grip on something I believed I had my arms around. We had a business psychologist who worked with top management at Estée Lauder, who helped when I needed someone to talk to. He'd say, "Off the record, you're never going to be happy here. You're never going to be able to do what you want." I wouldn't believe it.

Instead, I poured myself into new projects, still believing I could right the ship. I developed a line of eyeglasses and wrote another book. In 2014, Yahoo offered me a part-time position as editor in chief of their new online beauty magazine. I saw it as a cool, creative way to expand my reach and do what I love. When corporate refused to give me permission to join Yahoo, I explained it to them from a marketing perspective. We'd have a huge new audience to tell about my products, or any Estée Lauder products. They finally agreed to let me work one day a week at Yahoo's offices in Midtown because I threatened to leave if they didn't.

The project had legs. Yahoo hired Katie Couric for news, Joe Zee for fashion, Kerry Diamond for food, and Michele Promaul-ayko for health. I hired Henry Leutwyler to take pictures, his wife Ruba to be the creative director, and Joan Juliet Buck, former head of French *Vogue*, as a writer. The day we launched, Yahoo flew us to the Cannes Lions International Festival of Creativity. It was so exciting.

I loved the work. I interviewed fascinating people like Cate Blanchett, John Legend, and Jennifer Aniston. I had all these interesting, new projects. It invigorated me, and it brought opportunities for the brand. I felt like a PR machine. I was engaged creatively and learning a lot.

Sadly, it fell apart after a year or so. Yahoo was too disorganized. They hired a consultant to fix it, but eventually they decided to get rid of everyone but Joe Zee. The consultant called me and soft sold the change, but as soon as she hung up, she accidentally butt-dialed me. I sat there in disbelief, listening to her entire conversation about how they were going to fire me and all the other editors, then I called her back and said, "I heard everything. You are really lucky it was me and not someone else." I could have been vengeful, but it wasn't my style. That was the end of Yahoo.

A new team was in at the *Today* show and was making changes and cuts. They offered me a lesser position at the show, which, after fourteen years, hurt. I decided to stop doing it. I felt bad for a day or two, then I texted Elvis Duran's producer and said, "I have this crazy idea. Can I be your beauty and lifestyle editor?" He asked Elvis, who responded with a "Hell yeah!"

When things got tough at work, I pushed harder. In 2015, we launched the Be Who You Are campaign, promoting the belief that a woman is her most beautiful when she looks and feels like herself. We hired Katie Holmes as our first spokesmodel, and then Kate Upton. I felt that our product innovation was as good as ever, but our ad campaigns didn't look right. The pictures were retouched and inauthentic. Some of it was my fault. I hired the wrong people. Some of it was the constant pressure from corporate to make us look like every other brand. On top of all that, our marketing budgets were so low, we barely had the money to mount a proper campaign. We couldn't do anything on the scale we were used to. I had the idea to launch the campaign on Facebook Live, which had just come out, but the Wi-Fi was so bad in the office, the video kept cutting out.

Under pressure to be like all the other established brands, we lost our identity. Meanwhile, new brands were launching that reminded me of the cool, scrappy, unique, independent company we used to be. Glossier was making ads showing girls in messy buns with barely any makeup. I felt like they were doing my thing, while I was stuck in this corporate world I didn't believe in anymore. Estée Lauder was no longer the right place for me, but I still couldn't admit it. I kept complaining to Steven, kept calling Aunt Alice for advice, and kept trying to find the fix.

By the company's twenty-fifth anniversary in 2016, I was exhausted and still fighting. The day before attending a big party in London to celebrate the milestone, we had a disastrous meeting in my office. Veronika had put together a plan for a month's worth of social media content. She knew I wouldn't like it, but she also knew she had to appease her corporate bosses. After the presentation I said, "I hated every bit of that," and left feeling tense and upset.

Veronika and I didn't see each other again until we arrived in London the next day. I had found out that Estée Lauder called an off-site meeting without telling me. Veronika came to my room to find me in a fury.

"I'm going to fucking leave," I said.

"Listen, Bobbi," she said, "maybe you would be happier doing your own thing."

"Will you leave with me?" I asked.

Veronika had a family to support and needed her job and its benefits. She said she couldn't take the risk of following me out the door. It didn't matter. Despite my threats, I still couldn't walk away from my brand. Quite the opposite: I returned from London with new ideas of how to fix it. I met with the corporate team and told them exactly why I thought things weren't working and how I intended to get it back on track, including hiring a new president from outside the brand. I left the meeting with assurances that they'd get a headhunter and find someone.

After several weeks without hearing anything more about it, I realized the executives at Estée Lauder were just humoring me. I thought back to something Fred, my driver, who had been with me for many years, had told me earlier that year. "I gotta tell you," he said one morning on the drive into work, "I overheard one of the corporate guys on the phone talking about when they are going to fire you."

"Fred, stop," I said. "They won't do that."

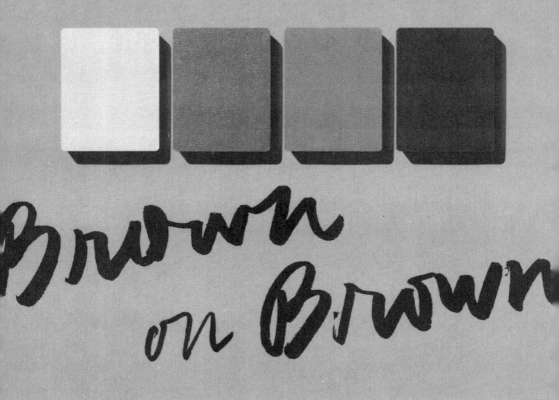

Brown
on Brown

CHAPTER THIRTY

FULL STOP

In October 2016, Estée Lauder's executive group president summoned me to the GM Building. Still unwilling to believe my problems had no solution, I thought he wanted to talk about the candidates they had found to replace our president. I entered his office to find him sitting with a woman I recognized from corporate.

"Sit down," she said.

I sat down.

"We're canceling your work contract," she said.

"Are you firing me?"

"No."

"It sounds like you are."

"We're taking you out of the day-to-day operations," she said. "We have a new proposal for you."

She handed me a piece of paper.

"I'm not reading this," I said.

"You have to."

"You just fired me. I don't have to do anything."

I put the paper down and left. I had heard enough. Canceling my work contract, taking me out of the day-to-day—this was firing by another name. I later learned that the proposal was for me to remain the face of the company without any power in running it for the same or more money.

Riding down in the elevator, I had the most bizarre sensation. A giant sense of relief came over me. All my angst and worry were gone—but just for one second. Then I took out my phone only to realize they had already locked me out of my Instagram and my email account. I was angry, shocked, and betrayed. I felt like a sucker for trusting these people.

As I walked out of the building, my first concern was Fred, my driver. I worried about him being out of a job. My second thought was *What am I going to do for Halloween?* Many of my neighbors had distinguished themselves in their fields, and it was our tradition to give out something special to kids on Halloween. The president of Scholastic gave out books. Yogi gave out signed baseball cards. I gave out lip gloss. I couldn't imagine not doing it, and now I couldn't do it.

I called Steven.

"I either quit or got fired," I said.

"I'm on my way into the city," he said. "Meet me for wine and oysters."

When I saw Steven, the first thing he said was "Are you okay?"

"I don't know," I said.

This company was my first baby. It was my identity. Other than my family, it was all I thought about. All of a sudden, it was gone.

"Well, I'm glad," he said. "I've been waiting a long time to have you back."

I realized then how hard it was for the people who loved me to see me suffer for so long, and how much I had been suffering. The day-to-day craziness of my schedule had insulated me from it. I'd had a lot of other places to put my focus. But I couldn't ignore it anymore. I had been miserable for a long, long time.

A few days later, I called Aunt Alice and told her I left Estée Lauder.

"What took you so long?" she said.

She had been advising me for a year that it was time to move on.

"So What, Now What?"

—Liz Murray

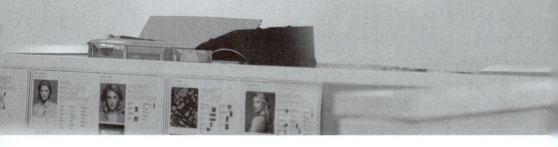

CHAPTER THIRTY-ONE

SHIT HAPPENS

I stayed at Estée Lauder for twenty-two years. Most of those years were joyous, creative, and invigorating. The ones near the end were tough, and the last year was miserable. When you have a streak like I did, it's hard to admit it's over. I loved our mission and our brand so much, but what I loved and missed most was the people.

Shit happens. The world changes. People change. The good times you thought would last end. If you're lucky, they end peacefully. Or they go down in flames. Either way, they end. Around the time I left Estée Lauder, many of the editors in chief I had known and worked with for so many years also got pushed out of their positions. The magazines brought in younger, less expensive, more digitally savvy people. It was a changing of the guard.

It hurts, and you need to admit it hurts. You need to be able to say, "I feel like a failure," to people who will listen and sympathize instead of responding. This was when I needed my posse, my true friends and family, the most. These were friends I'd met over the years in Montclair before they—or we—were anything. We raised our kids together, spent holidays together, and often traveled together. There were couples we'd known for more than thirty years—who'd become our community and family, and whose successes we cheered even as we all never forgot who we were. Who we still are.

I leaned on them, confided in them, and they were there for me, just as my family was.

And even as I was reeling, I realized it was vital to remember I had power. I couldn't control events, but I could control my attitude. Aunt Alice taught me that. My dad taught me that. It's how you respond that matters.

Don't get me wrong: when shit happens, it can leave you lost, unmoored, adrift. After leaving Estée Lauder, I didn't know what to do, but I also hadn't known how to start a company or what to do on Obama's trade commission or how to stand in front of an audience and give a speech. I hadn't known how to graciously tell a line full of people waiting for my autograph that I needed to use the bathroom or how to walk a red carpet next to Taylor Swift in an Oscar de la Renta dress. All of this I'd had to figure out in real time. And I had.

Shit happens. Be sad. Be angry. Be hurt, relieved, scared, and in doubt. Then do something about it.

" The hardest lesson I've learned:
Nothing is what you think it is, and you have to adapt.**"**

PART SEVEN

MAKE LEMONADE

CHAPTER THIRTY-TWO

OPTIONS

That night I was in shock. My besties came over with a bottle of tequila. We laughed, I cried, and they listened to me vent. It's times like these that reinforce how important your posse is. They returned the next night. After that I was ready for the next phase of grief, whatever it might be.

I didn't feel much of anything for a few days. As the shock wore off, I went through a ton of emotions. I was angry. I was sad. I was relieved. At times I felt excited and free for the first time in years. Other times I felt like someone had cut off my arms.

Steven supported me and listened to me over and over again,

as did my family and friends. Mickey Drexler, the then CEO of J. Crew, called every morning to check in. Richard Baker, who owns Saks, Neiman Marcus, and Bergdorf, checked on me. Sara Blakely, founder of Spanx, and Jo Malone, who had experienced similar things, also reached out. Marcia Kilgore, founder of Beauty Pie, offered me use of her labs. Those early and daily calls made all the difference at such a tough time.

Sadly, I couldn't talk to my work colleagues and friends who had experienced these last years with me. I was told Estée Lauder had warned my team not to communicate with me. If they got caught, they'd be fired. A few people disregarded this instruction and reached out anyway. Some would call from their kids' phones so they didn't get caught. And it was eye-opening to see who didn't call at all. I now understand they didn't want to jeopardize their jobs and careers, but I felt deserted and betrayed by many people I had hired and considered friends. They picked a side, and it hurt. Many of these relationships ended. Happily, I have since rekindled with a few key people. It took a while, though.

While I grieved, Steven dealt with Estée Lauder's lawyers. They explained to him the offer I had refused to read, hoping I would accept it. The company wanted me to be a figurehead but not be involved in creating or marketing the cosmetic products. For years, whenever they'd wanted to buy some cool, indie company, they'd trot me out like a show pony to talk about how great it was working for Estée Lauder. They still wanted that. They just didn't want everything else that came with me.

I refused to sit by, a powerless observer, and watch the formulas my team and I had worked so hard to create, and the messages we had put so much time and energy into, be ruined. I couldn't see myself smiling for the cameras as the company became something I didn't believe in. Estée Lauder also demanded I sign a non-disparagement agreement. I was so insulted. I don't react well to anyone telling me what I can or cannot do.

"No fucking way," I told Steven.

"Are you sure?" he said. "It's a lot of money, and you don't have to do much."

I was sure.

They then arbitrarily blocked my unexercised stock options, which were worth a lot of money, thinking I would cave. Steven coolly replied that "Bobbi is insulted that the company would attempt to take these [options] away from her . . . Sadly, I don't see any alternative to litigation."

The next day they reinstated the options. But it was too late. The damage was done. We immediately redeemed the options and sold the stock. I'm not sure the new executives ever understood me. I wanted no association with them. I was finally free.

For the first time in nearly forty years, I had nothing to do and nowhere to go. No driver to take me to my office in the morning. (Fred kept driving but lost his biggest client.) No meetings to attend, no products to create or discuss, nothing to promote. Our house was quiet. I had no kids at home to feed, bathe, and mother. I was uncertain about the future and what I wanted to do.

Doing nothing wasn't an option. When I first signed my contract, I assumed I'd be ready to retire by now. But as it turned out, the word "retire" doesn't fit into my vocabulary. My dear friend Dick Ebersol walked away from forty-two years at NBC and loved his life not working. He encouraged me to try it. Another friend, Roger Dolden, ex-CFO of L'Oréal, preached the same. But I wanted to do something. I just was not sure what. It was an uncertain, nervous, yet exciting time for me.

I finally had the time to really explore. I began scheduling random meals and meetings like I did when I first moved to New York. I'd meet friends for lunch downtown, then wander around the city, checking out the hip little stores and cool smaller makeup brands. I said yes to anyone who reached out, doing things I wouldn't have had time to do before. I spoke at the Indie Beauty conference, where I saw my younger self in the founders. I found their energy infectious.

I stayed busy and started to figure it out, while still dealing with an emotional roller coaster. I went to see my functional chiropractor, who helped me release much negative energy. It sounds crazy, but it works. I took yoga classes from my friend, who was also a life coach. I didn't know what a life coach was. He offered me a free session and we spent an hour talking. It was very therapeutic to get my thoughts out. He was a good listener and gave me great practical advice, and we discussed goals for me to achieve before our next session: call people, make appointments, get up early to exercise.

One day I visited the Apple Store hoping to keep my phone number but separate my account from Lauder. The girl who waited on me spent four hours trying to figure out how to do this seemingly impossible task. She never gave up, like many people would have done. She had no clue who I was, but she worked with me until she figured it out. I offered her a job. Even though I had no idea what I was going to do, I knew I would need an assistant to do it. She started the next week.

On a call with Richard Baker, I told him what had happened. "This is the best news," he said. "Come work with me." He offered to let me create my own pop-up shops in Lord & Taylor. I needed Lauder's permission (I was still governed by my non-compete), which they gave me, along with a list of things I couldn't do. This wasn't the same as running my own brand, but it did give me a reason to build a new team and got me into a project I had no idea how to do. That excited me. I had my Apple Store assistant Michelle; my PR neighbor Lynette; my ex-Lauder assistant turned business lead Tara; Yogi's granddaughter Gretchen; and a fashion stylist I met on Instagram, Ali. With this small posse, I built the justBobbi shops at Lord & Taylor.

justBobbi was a curated lifestyle and beauty shop. I filled it with anything and everything I loved from other brands and from the Lord & Taylor store itself. As part of the deal, Lauder had me include Bobbi Brown Cosmetics. We just dove in, which I loved. We brought in some funky items from Karl Lagerfeld, some cool Parker Thatch bags and Hudson's Bay striped blankets, as well as some vitamins and supplements.

Lord & Taylor was a great partner. Richard understood me and my creativity. He's a brilliant businessman, super creative, and kind of crazy. That's a winning combination. He gave me a team to execute my vision. Anything I asked for, he said, "Sure, why not?" The stores got a lot of buzz, and stories about my new venture started popping up in the magazines. We created events and eventually rolled out to four or five other locations. The contract was originally for six months and was renewed for another six months. It was exhilarating to have people who had the same wide-eyed optimism I did and were fearless, like me. Unfortunately, after one year, Lord

& Taylor closed their stores, so our team brought the justBobbi concept in-house and created a website to support it.

Meanwhile, few people outside my close circle knew what I was going through. Lauder executives waited until the Friday before Christmas to formally announce our split. I was on the way to a Stevie Wonder concert when the CEO called. I asked him why he called me.

"I wanted to know if you saw the announcement and if you're happy with it," he said.

"What are you talking about?" I said. "You fired me!"

"No, I didn't fire you. I gave you a new opportunity."

I was angry and told him what I had been holding in for seven years: how he had sucked the soul out of not just my brand but the whole company. I didn't curse, but I spewed. Then I said, "If you think I'm not going back into the beauty industry I love, you are mistaken."

"I'd love to get together after the New Year and talk about it," he said.

"I don't ever want to talk to you again," I said.

I hung up and watched Stevie Wonder perform. I felt good.

That year, I turned sixty. I published my ninth book, *Beauty from the Inside Out*, which focused more on health and wellness than makeup. I did the whole book tour in sneakers, a blazer, and jeans. I still felt a sense of loss, but I also felt a certain freedom to be myself in ways I couldn't before.

As sadness began to lift, frustration set in. Under the terms of the twenty-five-year non-compete clause, I couldn't publicly be associated with another makeup brand until 2020, which was four and a half years away. When someone tells me I can't do something, it makes me more determined to do it. My mind was filled with ideas. I considered making a brown eye pencil and launching it on Etsy without my name attached. I considered starting a brand called Nameless—we actually reserved the rights to it—and launching without telling anyone it was me. Steven said, "Just wait." But I didn't want to wait.

I have a dear friend who ran an investment firm that had just bought Avon. They didn't know what to do with it. He called and said, "If anyone can fix this, you can." I was intrigued. Avon is the original women's empowerment brand. I knew I could lean into that. It seemed they needed me. I'd get to bring in the best team and be given the resources to do what I wanted to do.

My team put together a deck, which I thought was cool and compelling. In the middle of our presentation to the top brass at Avon, the chairman of the board got up and stood behind me, put his hand on my shoulder, and asked in a pompous and misogynistic way, "Little lady, have you ever run a movie studio?"

"No," I said. "But I have built a billion-dollar beauty brand."

Mic drop.

After a few more meetings with Avon, I knew it wasn't going to work. Still, it was a great experience. It gave me something to think about and the opportunity to ideate how I would build a business, and it also made me feel good knowing somebody thought I was worthy.

I needed these boosts of confidence. Around that time, we flew our close friends down to the Bahamas for Steven's sixtieth birthday. While we partied on the beach, the chef told me what a big fan he was.

"You're great," he said.

I hung my head and said, "Nah, not anymore."

"Dude, look at me," he said. "You got this."

I smiled and thought, "Yeah, I got this!"

"You got this" became my mantra. I put it on mugs, pencils, coasters, and other items we sold at Lord & Taylor, and eventually online.

I got this! Why? I had nothing left to prove. I didn't need the money. I had earned and received plenty of accolades and awards. Many people would have just let go, but I was determined to create something new. I didn't know what, but I had to do it.

Since Dylan's birth, I have worn a charm from the jeweler Helen Ficalora with his initials on it. I added a D for Dakota and one for Duke, and a peace sign for me. Around my sixtieth birthday, I got an S for Steven. While shopping at the store, I saw an ampersand charm, and it sparked something. I needed it. The ampersand meant my story wasn't over. I bought it and had "10.20," the date my non-compete ended, engraved on it. Though it seemed like a lifetime to have to wait, whenever I felt anxious, I'd touch the necklace and think, *You got this.*

CHAPTER THIRTY-THREE

THE GEORGE

Though I couldn't work in makeup, I needed to do something. The day I left the brand Steven said, "I just bought this building. I was thinking of turning it into condos or apartments, but what do you think of turning it into a hotel?"

Why not?

We started kicking around ideas. When I traveled with the company, I stayed at fancy hotels with butlers. But when Steven and I traveled alone, we chose small, boutique hotels that had a more casual and high-touch vibe. We wanted to create a place that we'd want to stay at, something cool, comfortable, and design focused, with the most welcoming staff, a memorable customer experience, and perks galore.

The building was a mess. Built in 1902, it had spent the last years as a rooming house. He completely gutted it and created thirty-one new rooms, each with its own unique character. Steven had another project nearby, an old factory he was renovating into offices. We took it over and used it as a space to experiment. We would buy random furniture, rugs, art, accessories, and linens, and have them delivered to our "lab." We are both very visual, so in this way, we could see what we liked, what went well together, and what would make enough of an impact to splurge on before actually putting it in the George. It was a passion project. But not overspending while still making a profit has always been important to both of us.

I loved seeing Steven's creativity in action. He could walk into an empty room and envision how it should look, from the paint color to the furniture layout to the wall decorations. I gave my opinions too. It's not always easy to work with your husband. Steven and I are both opinionated and strong-willed. Luckily, we have very similar aesthetics, and we've been married long enough to know when to compromise.

While Steven's team, subcontractors, and crew rebuilt the building, I began arranging collaboration deals with some of my favorite companies, like Casper for mattresses and sheets, Dyson for hair dryers, and Nespresso for in-room service. I also reached out to Susan Feldman, cofounder of One Kings Lane, and worked out a fun collaboration. We curated furniture for the first-floor lobby and library, and we advised our guests that if they liked the furniture, they could buy it online. Our teams worked together and discussed carpeting, paints, etc. We collectively worked on logos and creating a cool hotel brand.

For the George's opening in spring 2018, we sent invitations to travel editors, influencers, and VIPs. We hired a great photographer and did a beautiful photo shoot. The photos began to appear online and in all the magazines. These magazines knew I had left my brand but they didn't know what I was doing, so this was a big deal. We got great stories about the pending opening in *Travel + Leisure* and *Vogue*, among others.

A few days before our opening party, we still weren't ready. But a deadline is a great motivator. We ran frantically through all the rooms, making finishing touches, doing whatever we had to do to open the doors on time. I brought over pillows, books, and art from my house and barely had more than fifteen minutes to shower and get ready for the party. The hotel showed really well. For the opening, we invited the press in the morning, and friends and family at night. After we completed the few things left to fix, Steven and I officially became hoteliers.

We had a few early hiccups. After we felt the initial company we hired to clean the hotel was expensive and sloppy, we ended up hiring our personal housekeeper, who was up for the challenge. She incorporated, built, and trained a staff, and took over. I could trust her. After working with me for so long, she knows how I like things to look.

Not going to lie, we had more than a bunch of hiccups and had to recalibrate a few times with hires. It finally came together. Our staff cares so deeply about the hotel and guests that we can be hands-off on the day-to-day. I'm proud that it has become a well-oiled machine and has received many accolades and a few prestigious awards. It's been fun to host many a celebrity who is in town for a movie or event. And I particularly love to drop in and chat with the guests and ask why they are there. So many great stories—and one such guest led to a Williams Sonoma collab between the George and Williams Sonoma.

Around this time, I received an invitation to teach a master class at the first-ever India Makeup Show in Mumbai and Delhi. It was a big commitment, and I said yes.

For this class I needed to use makeup, but I didn't want to use Bobbi Brown. Emotionally, I didn't want to be near it, so I had to re-create my makeup bag. I pulled together tons of makeup I bought, and reached out to a few makeup brands for more. I packed a large suitcase for the trip, and hopped on the plane with Steven for a two-week adventure. It was a huge undertaking, without a support team, without a posse, makeup assistant, or PR. The people who hired me took care of everything, including providing me with a local team.

India was eye-opening and inspirational. It is the most interesting, beautiful country. So many people, sights, and smells. Mumbai makes Times Square look like a small town. People move in every direction, cars, bicycles, motorcycles, animals, even rickshaws. You don't hear many horns honking. It's total chaos, but somehow it works.

The makeup shows were on consecutive weekends, and during the week we visited Agra and Jaipur. On my sixty-first birthday, we stayed at a beautiful hotel overlooking the Taj Mahal. It was incredible. When I arrived I asked for a cocktail and was informed it wasn't possible due to an Indian holiday when no alcohol was allowed. Steven somehow got access to the basement of the hotel and secured libations, determined to celebrate with me on this occasion. Magical.

I didn't know many of the Indian celebrities at the shows—people like Bollywood actress Malaika Arora, hairstylist Adhuna Bhabani, and beauty influencer Mira Rajput Kapoor—but I loved working with them, standing on that stage, and doing what I do best: connecting with people through makeup and demystifying the world of beauty for normal women. It was me and my bag of makeup, just like the old days. The experience helped me realize I don't need the power and influence of a large corporation. I just need to be me.

Soon thereafter, another call came in. MasterClass reached out for me to create and produce their first-ever makeup tutorial. MasterClass produces digital classes from industry experts on a range of topics such as art, design, and sports. It was an honor to be selected. This turned out to be one of the greatest experiences of my career. I put everything I had into it. The teams were top-notch and the biggest crew I had ever worked with. Shot in our home studio, 18 Label, with three beautiful models, plus my own hairdresser and stylist and makeup assistants, we shot for eight hours a day. We filled the tables with a flat lay of all the makeup you could possibly need or dream of. And the pressure was on to perform. Fortuitously I was using these little lab samples of formulas I'd been developing as a curiosity to see what I could make that was different. And they worked like a charm on camera. These little pots and jars would eventually be launched in the new company. What an incredible way to test the formulas!

I still felt impatient waiting for my non-compete clause to end, but these opportunities helped. I think I needed this break to clear the clutter in my head. Plus, I had other things to keep me busy. In August 2019, Hurricane Dorian struck the Bahamas. Steven and I have a vacation home on one of the smaller islands, and we watched helplessly from Montclair as our community was nearly destroyed. Steven immediately began calling everyone we knew in our community, until finally getting a hold of someone. "How can we help?"

We heard about a few employees whose home had been destroyed, and we offered to host them in New Jersey. They were brothers and they asked if they could bring their family. We said yes, not realizing that their family included four brothers, two parents, one sister, three babies, three partners, and one uncle—about fourteen people in all. Steven and I looked at each other and with no hesitation said, "Of course everyone is welcome."

Our community in the Bahamas got them to Florida, but they couldn't fly to us because most had had their passports and IDs destroyed. So Steven arranged a private plane for them.

They arrived in Montclair a week after the storm. Our new family was still in shock, but they were very stoic and gracious. We found room for them wherever we could: in our house, at the hotel, at some of Steven's other properties. We'd get up in the morning and pick our way through the bodies sleeping on every available bed and couch. It was a phenomenal experience getting to know them. I realized how similar we are, even as different as we are.

This family had lost everything. They needed medicine and doctors, phones, bras, sneakers, socks, toothbrushes, towels, shirts, and pants. We made spreadsheets of the sizes and needs of each person. Our community and friends were unbelievably supportive. Rutgers

University donated Rutgers athletic clothes, and I posted pictures of the family wearing them on my Instagram account. Wacoal donated bras and underwear. The more we asked for, the more we received. Local doctors offered their services, restaurants dropped off food; it was an amazing outpouring of love. Neighbors delivered cribs, formula, bottles, clothes, and food. Another angel provided them all with cell phone service, and other companies donated clothing. Steven provided a two-family house for them to live in and the community furnished it. They stayed for a year and became part of our family. The experience made us all richer.

By the end of 2019, I felt like my best self. I felt free. I no longer had to play a character for a large company. I said goodbye to uncomfortable shoes and too-tight clothes. I realized I had the power to say no. Every invitation had to pass a high bar, and if I did decide to go somewhere, I went as just Bobbi. I had been striving my whole life for this confidence. It came to me in stages, but I began to feel like I had finally figured it out.

CHAPTER THIRTY-FOUR

EVOLUTION

I've always known that beauty and health are intertwined. I believe how you feel impacts the way you look. This concept inspired many of the activations while at Bobbi Brown Cosmetics, but it also reflected my life. I had been on my own personal journey to improve my health and beauty.

At sixty-one years old, I didn't care what other people thought I was supposed to look like. There was always pressure to look younger, but surgery or injections were not my thing. I actually wanted to see a natural face at any age. Lines are just a normal thing. However, in my quest for feeling better, I know I look better when I am paying attention to both.

In 2017, my sister, Linda, had become a health coach through the Institute for Integrative Nutrition, and she recommended I try it, thinking I would find the curriculum beneficial. It captivated me. I was so into learning, and now I finally had the time to do it. The courses were digital, which allowed me to study at my own pace. Whenever I had a free moment, I'd go into our backyard sauna and "attend class." As someone who really can't sit still, being in the sauna was perfect for me. I had to sit still but could easily focus on my iPad with the content.

The course taught me a ton— it taught me that everyone is unique and that what's right for one person isn't necessarily right for another. They call it bio-individuality. I'd read about the vegan diet one lesson plan and the next read about the protein-based Paleo diet. At the end of each lesson, I was sure I wanted to eat as I'd just been taught! By the end of my studies, I realized I didn't want to label myself. I simply want to put good, whole food in my body, be intuitive about what I eat, and not feel guilty if I eat dessert or have chocolate now and then. Oh, and more importantly, your thoughts matter!

I began making subtle changes—replacing my old cleaning products with chemical-free organic products. I checked every ingredient at the grocery store before purchasing. I made sure exercise was part of my regular routine as well—but I realized something was missing: FUN.

I thought long and hard about what would be "fun" for me. And then it came to me—dance. I love to dance. If there's a good DJ at a party, you can't get me off the floor. I really wasn't very good at it but that never stopped me. I decided to sign up for lessons and asked a local fitness instructor for privates. That's how I started taking hip-hop with Lloyd twice a week. I loved it. I got better. Funnily enough, I couldn't follow all his routines so he let me go free and followed me while working on technique. Lloyd made little videos of my lessons and posted them on my Instagram and they were a hit. Soon Lloyd developed a booming business.

I got invited to a Flo Rida concert—a very small thing, maybe one hundred people in the audience—and I told him about my love of hip-hop and dancing. In the middle of his concert, he said, "Hey, where's my gal Bobbi Brown? Come up and dance." Duke, a teenager at the time, couldn't believe I actually did it. Another time, I got called onstage to dance with Salt-N-Pepa. I pushed it. But that's what life's about. Pushing the limits and having fun while doing it.

EVOLUTION_18

My family said I'd never complete the Institute for Integrative Nutrition degree—but I did. I finished, I passed, I was a certified health coach. And if you know me, it makes perfect sense. Another way to be a teacher and empower people to be them, but better. And the journey would stick with me as I would soon enter into a new business around wellness—Evolution_18.

Around this time, Gretchen, on my team, had a friend who worked at a vitamin supplier and manufacturer. She suggested I build on my recent degree and book, and pitch the boss a concept for a health-and-wellness vitamin brand based on the idea that beauty comes from the inside out. Why not? That was the concept and title of my newest book.

The idea was to create health products using quality ingredients, products that tasted delicious and had beauty benefits, and sell them at an affordable price. The manufacturer understood my vision and signed on as a partner. We came up with some great products that I thought people would love: a tea to take away bloating, a water-soluble tablet to combat skin flaking and dryness, chewable gummies packed with biotin to strengthen hair and nails, and a delicious chocolate protein powder shake that filled you up.

We named the company Evolution_18—the number eighteen means "life" in Hebrew, which felt right, and it's also the address of our photo studio. We launched it in Walmart. I was just as excited to open at Walmart as I had been twenty-five years earlier when Bobbi Brown Essentials opened at Bergdorf Goodman. I thought this new venture could be big. This time I had the power of my name and my reputation, as well as Walmart's large platform. But I had no idea what to expect, not in the luxury market.

We got to work. Funnily enough the business deal was similar to my deal with the chemist when I launched lipsticks. Fifty percent cut of the profits, the partner supplied the products, and we would market and run operations. The partner had connections in this world, and he opened his doors. Our team was inexperienced but passionate and willing to work. Every day we ideated and came up with formulas we wanted to create. There was a lot of tasting and it was not easy when I was adamant the formulas had to taste good, be clean, and do what we promised. When I think back on those days, it was interesting and frustrating. Interesting because I always love doing things I have no idea how to do, but frustrating because I did not have an experienced team.

It was very humbling to discover that many of the people standing in line on our opening day had never heard of me or my old company. They simply wanted the free samples we were handing out. Still, I approached the new company the same way I did with my original cosmetics start-up. We organized marketing shoots with beautiful models and brought in content creators. Boots, the health-and-beauty retailer in the UK, offered to carry our products. Walmart believed in it too. They seemed excited about trying something new and dedicated resources to promote it.

We launched strong and the Walmart teams were all in. We combined our social media efforts and did a press tour. It was fun being back involved with a project I was passionate about. As expected, I was paying attention to the things I cared about—product, marketing, PR—but I didn't pay a lot of attention to the books: numbers, contracts, etc. . . . And soon realized the products were not getting replenished in-store and the cardboard testers were beginning to fall apart. And so was my focus. I began to fade. Eventually when I asked someone to look at the state of the business, it was brought to my attention that it wasn't worth doing.

In the spring of 2019, I attended a natural-food show in California and was excited to witness and meet vendors offering healthy foods; vitamins; and natural, clean makeup. As I walked around, I noticed a tiny table of cosmetics from a lab in New Mexico. I went over and started touching and testing the samples, like I always do. I liked the product and introduced myself. I don't think they knew who I was, but they let me take a bunch of samples.

I fell in love with one of the lipsticks. It felt different, and the formula used clean ingredients. And I needed something to give away on Halloween. I ordered fifteen hundred of the lipsticks and printed labels that said "Batch 18" (based on our photo studio, 18 Label Studios, and Evolution_18).

After Halloween, I was bombarded with people asking where they could buy this lipstick. Apparently people loved it. I couldn't sell it yet, but with only one year left on my non-compete contract, I was excited to know that people liked what I liked. It gave me the enthusiasm to work on a new concept for a new brand.

I didn't know I was about to do it all over again. We began to perfect the lipstick and to develop other products. I didn't know what to name this new company or what it would be, but I was excited about the products. We had a list of twenty-five hundred ingredients banned by the European Union, and decided we wouldn't use any of them. I hoped to make the ultimate clean no-makeup makeup.

Around this time, I asked a couple of finance friends for help with the struggling Evolution_18. After a deep dive into our numbers and contracts, they advised me to walk away. I realized my involvement and name alone wouldn't guarantee success. The product has to be great, the team experienced, and the marketing relevant to the sales channel. Another opportunity to learn and grow.

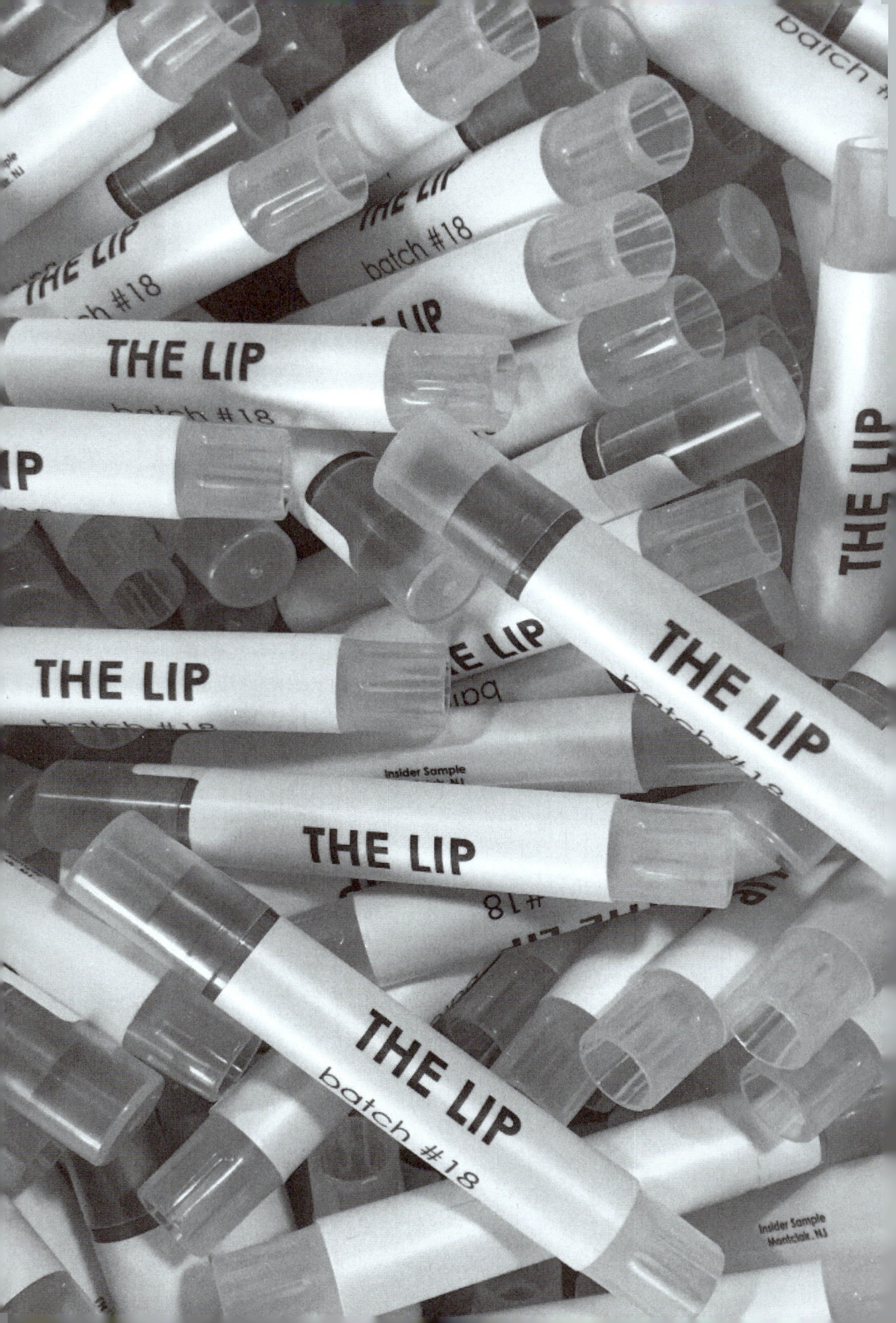
THE LIP
batch #18
THE LIP
THE LIP
THE LIP
batch #18
Insider Sample
THE LIP
THE LIP
batch #18
Insider Sample
Montclair, NJ

CHAPTER THIRTY-FIVE

DO YOU BELIEVE IN MIRACLES?

Patient, I am not.

Optimistic and creative, I am.

I was finally ready to start again—the same but totally different. I realized I just wasn't done. I still have things to teach and products to create. I began collecting pictures of what this new brand could be. These included images of faces I did with photographer Ben Ritter, whom I'd hired at Yahoo beauty. His lighting was perfect, because it made the minimal makeup I used look glowy on the models instead of flat. To me, those pictures were revolutionary. They were simple and clean. I'd felt that the later photographs at Bobbi Brown weren't as authentic looking as I had hoped and were way too retouched. These photos were the opposite. They looked fresh. They were me.

I also took inspiration from Phoebe Philo's work with Céline. Phoebe is a fashion designer, and I recognized myself in much of what she did, from her minimal designs and tonal palettes to models who were perfectly imperfect and wore little to no visible makeup. I also imagined a downtown, relaxed vibe. I always loved the coolness of the skateboard company Supreme's hoodies and bolts of red in their logos. I described the vibe I wanted for my new company as Céline meets Supreme.

I didn't want a partner for the new venture, and I have never taken investor money. The entire series—A, B, C—was foreign to me. This time, I didn't want to lose control over even a small percentage of the ownership. Steven, ever the voice of reason, said, "We can do this ourselves. We can invest our own money and see what happens." He gave me a sum with which he was comfortable starting this new venture. He moved us from our small storage-closet office to a bigger one around the corner with brick walls and cement floors. He was the "You got this, I believe in you" guy in my ear. He wholeheartedly believes in me. He is a true business partner who sets up everything for success, whether it's bank accounts, accounting, hiring the right team, building the board (we went with two of our besties with deep experience and big hearts), or just understanding what it takes to make a venture a success—and not only from a business standpoint, but also from a human standpoint. There are issues that arise that are part business, part emotion, and are all real. It's a must for anyone in business to understand how essential this is.

Investing our own money meant we'd be free from outside opinions and control, which sounded great after my last experience. This freedom was exactly what I craved. It was simple, at least in my mind. I wanted to launch the brand the day my non-compete with Estée Lauder ended. The marketing and the products would showcase the ultimate no-makeup makeup, my way. And the formulas and products would be clean.

To make clean products, I invited the New Mexico lab owner to meet me in New York, and we placed an initial order. They didn't have the capacity to make everything we needed, so we found other companies to manufacture other products for us.

One of my first product ideas was a whipped foundation, creamy and opaque with skin-tone color. I hired my first full-time employee, Chrissy, to lead product development, and together we visited a lot of different labs. After many false starts, Chrissy told me about a lab she knew that we hadn't tried yet.

I explained to this new lab what I wanted. When the samples arrived, I opened the jar and saw this sheer concoction. "This isn't what I wanted," I said. I dipped my fingers in it anyway, rubbed it on my cheeks, looked in the mirror, and suddenly looked so much better. "Oh my God! This is a miracle!" It wasn't what I was expecting, but I loved it. That became the first product. We called it Miracle Balm.

The problem was the new lab couldn't make it clean. We kept searching until we found a lab that could. Then we re-created the balm with clean ingredients and came up with four tints: Au Naturel,

Bronze, Tawny, and Dusty Rose. All the while passing out tiny samples to my friends—who begged for more.

Next we worked on filling out the line. We found a lab that was able to make an ultra-black dense mascara that could be labeled clean. We couldn't believe it. We created a beautiful sparkle eye shadow formula that looked like transparent glass and didn't get into lines, as well as a non-gooey, sheer lip gloss with peppermint essence that was not at all like traditional glosses. We made an eye shadow called Just a Sec, because when I first tried it, I dipped my finger in it, put it on my eyelid, and said, "Well, that only took a second." We made a face pencil with a clear base and tint that keeps it from looking chalky on the skin. Two years later, we developed a foundation that didn't require moisturizer and didn't dry down into lines and crevices of the face. We called that one What the Foundation because the first time I tried it, it felt so good and I looked so good, I yelled out, "What the fuck?!"

Without all the corporate layers, things were simpler. I didn't have to get approval for my ideas, and since we were not in retail, I didn't have a timeline to consider. I'd think of something, talk to Chrissy about it, and if she and the other staff liked it, we made it. I didn't care what a market analysis would say. Only one question mattered: Do we love the product?

I was having fun again. I had once invented the no-makeup makeup look. Now I had the chance to perfect it and to modernize it. I knew the business. I understood how makeup was made, used, photographed, marketed, and sold. Plus, I was a formulator. I had taught myself by blending other companies' products and turning them into a single product that would be easy for anyone to apply.

I took everything I had learned in a lifetime of beauty and distilled it for the new company.

I also knew what I didn't know. I knew makeup. I was less interested in operations and finance. We put together a company board with Steven as chairman, our friend Gary Fuhrman—Estée Lauder's investment banker back in 1995, and Steven's longtime business partner, who had the background we needed and was our biggest cheerleader—and Lisa Gersh, former CEO of Martha Stewart Living and Goop, and cocreator of the Oxygen network. They were among our closest friends, and both believed in me, supported my vision, and brought in skills we needed.

At the beginning of 2020, October seemed far, far away. We had to keep the project under wraps until then. Somehow, though, Estée Lauder found out about what we were doing. Their lawyers contacted Steven, wanting to arbitrate our dispute. We had planned for this possibility. The new company was named Just Steven LLC, and I didn't own any of it. We had our friend, the well-known women's rights attorney Nancy Erika Smith, on retainer, along with a crisis PR firm. Our response to their demands was that we had no issues to arbitrate or even discuss. Steven's law degree came in handy again. He believed they were trying to intimidate us with their demands, and we called their bluff. We never heard from them or their lawyers again. And with Steven at my side, it took the angst away. All he ever has to say to me is "don't worry" (funny, it's the song we walked down the aisle to—Bobby McFerrin, "Don't Worry Be Happy").

CHAPTER THIRTY-SIX

THE YEAR
THE EARTH
STOOD STILL

In March 2020, I gave a speech at Syracuse University, where Duke was in his senior year. While there, we heard rumors of a dangerous new virus and its rapid spread. Duke and I talked about it, thinking the fear was overblown. It came as quite a shock when I got back to Montclair and learned Syracuse had canceled classes and shut down.

When Covid hit, Steven and I retreated to our house in the Hamptons. Duke packed his truck and came to hunker down with us. Cody and Payal (his girlfriend at the time) came—followed by nephew Jeremy a few weeks later. Dylan and Kim took over our Montclair home and were occasional visitors. We devoured the news. We all thought the lockdown might last two weeks and gave a collective groan. How were we going to do this for two weeks?

We built a new society inside our little Hamptons pod. We had to learn to work around each other. Cody and Payal had a successful physical therapy business, which they had to move online. Steven had his development company, sports complexes, hotel, TV studio, and event space to lead. I was trying to launch a new brand. Dylan and Kim both had full-time jobs, and Duke sadly graduated from college on our couch and didn't get to go to Europe on spring break as planned. It seemed every room had someone on Zoom. I'd film an Instagram Live in the kitchen, only to have Steven walk in on my shot.

"Dude, I'm live," I'd say, exasperated.

"So what? It's lunchtime."

"Say hi to Steven, everyone," I'd say while he rooted around in the fridge behind me.

It was a strange and scary time. We were as terrified as everyone was of getting sick. As the lockdown went from two weeks to two months, we struggled to stay sane and hopeful. But now, when I look back, I realize what a special time it was. All these amazing family moments were happening as the world was coming apart. My kids were living under the same roof for the first time in more than a decade. I got to spend so much quality time with them, and really got to know them as adults.

Here's a little bit more about each of them. Dylan was always the serious one. He was born with an even personality and brains to match. We called him the professor or "all-ologist," because he seems to have the answer to everything. Was he always right or just so convincing he appeared so? By the Covid year, he had become a well-read and highly capable young man and a graduate of Stanford University with two degrees, and worked for a start-up. And quite the sourdough baker.

Cody always wanted to just be normal. He never liked the trappings that came with having famous and successful parents. Cody has always been a powerhouse athlete, even in kindergarten. He walks to his own drumbeat and becomes the best at what he does. Often, he's self-taught and laser focused, and he doesn't stop until he's ready for the next subject, sport, or challenge. He was recently named CEO of Jones Road—he demonstrated to everyone he was the best candidate for the title.

Duke, my forever baby, is definitely the cherry on my sundae. Creative and opinionated, he graduated with an art degree in photography, and I was convinced he'd be a creative director (now he works with the family investment office). He has his finger on the pulse of art, brands, and pop culture, loves the outdoors, and is always up for an adventure. He is an incredibly loyal friend, and is also often the family chef, along with his brother Dylan (lucky for him, I'm the Muttler, cleaning up after dinner).

During our quarantine, I got a chance to know my future daughters-in-law better. Dylan's wife, Kim, is wonderfully strong and smart, with a keen eye on fashion and popular culture, and is my zeitgeist to all that's cool. The bonus is that the California Holland family is now part of ours. Dylan and Kim's wedding in Mexico, which had to wait until the end of quarantine, was right out of the pages of *Vogue*. Cody's wife, Payal, is strong, smart, capable, is an incredible cook, and has a great mind for business. Their wedding, also during the pandemic, was a stunning Indian-Jewish celebration. Indian culture is so rich. It's been incredible to get to experience it and become close with not only Payal's family, but the entire extended Patel clan: aunties, cousins, and friends. We are so lucky to have them.

An added bonus was our nephew Jeremy coming to stay with us. The deep, long conversations were so great, with nothing but time on our hands. I'll never get that back. It was great having Jeremy. He became a buffer to some family dynamics, and has a special bond with every person in the family. Plus, it's hard to say no to an aunt so whenever I asked him for a favor he'd say yes. Somehow, for the sons, it was much easier to refuse me. Jeremy met his future wife, Brittany, at the end of the pandemic, and just like that, our family has grown again. Now I get the pleasure of hosting everyone at Thanksgiving!

We could have filmed a cooking show during this time. My family comprises foodies and talented chefs. The meals were epic, and the cocktails and wine flowed. We walked for hours on end with nowhere to go, having life conversations that might not have happened otherwise. We made a list of chores that no one really followed. Without a housekeeper, hairdresser, or assistant, it was a new world. I started coloring my hair at home, until one day Duke offered to help. He said he had watched people do it on Instagram. Eventually, we had a local hairdresser come to our backyard with a mask on to cut and color our hair when we needed it. Steven, who can't stay in one place and is fearless, always did the grocery shopping—and we'd holler at him when he put the grocery bags directly on the kitchen counter. I waited for them to air out on the porch overnight. Cody and Payal were the first to adopt a puppy and add to the mix of our and Dylan's dogs. Then Duke adopted a rescue and I fell in love with a runt at the shelter. Now we had five dogs between us. Every day was a party.

Steven and I bonded with local friends who were also in the Hamptons and in similar situations. I began to look forward to weekly Zoom cocktails with them. Eventually, sometime after the first or second vaccine, we began to socialize outside. I'll never forget the first time we had dinner on someone's porch. We were scared but we braved it and no one caught anything. In April, the first year of lockdown, my friends threw me a surprise birthday party on the street in front of my house, with gifts and cocktails. Everyone stayed far apart from each other, and my favorite gifts were toilet paper and hand sanitizer. Eventually we went on a friend's boat and ate dinner outside. Later that year we celebrated Steven's 64th birthday at an outdoor dinner with our friends. It was December, so we sat huddled beneath heaters, wrapped in heavy coats and blankets. Those were the days.

The lockdown also gave me valuable perspective on the new business I was trying to get off the ground. My beauty routine, like most women, changed dramatically during the pandemic. With nowhere to go and no one to see, I wasn't wearing any makeup. I'd turn the camera on to film an Instagram Live and think, *I look like shit.* So I'd rub a little test product I was developing on my face, and it felt like a secret weapon. It made me feel good and look way better. We named it Miracle Balm. I created the hashtag #hownottolooklikeshit. This emphasized the mission and philosophy of this new brand: when you feel good, you look good.

I gave mini samples of Miracle Balm to my friends, and they'd call me and say, "I just love this stuff." They'd come to my house wearing a mask, and I'd throw it to them from my porch. When people began braving the pandemic to get more of the new makeup, I knew I was onto something special.

My team couldn't meet in person, so we worked on Zoom. I hired the still-life photographer Jon Paterson, who was my favorite from the Yahoo days, and Ben Ritter, my fashion and beauty photographer, for a photo shoot in my back yard. For extra caution, we booked a doctor to give Covid tests onsite. I called a few models who lived nearby to attend. I also wanted an older model to represent a different age group. I had a vision of someone with salt-and-pepper hair who would photograph well. One day I was shopping at a local farm stand and saw this tall, beautiful woman with salt-and-pepper hair piled on her head working the register.

"Excuse me, can you take off your mask?" I asked.

"Why?"

"I'm Bobbi Brown, and I'm looking for a model for a shoot."

Her name was Shauna. She was stunning and perfect for what I was looking for. She looked so good in the pictures, we continued to book her in the future. Eventually, she got the modeling agency Wilhelmina to represent her.

"I don't want to work at the farm stand anymore, I want to be a customer," she said.

Shauna—and her story—was exactly what I wanted this brand to embody, fearless women with interesting features: freckles, gaps in their teeth, strong noses, and beautiful well-lived faces. I love a naturally aged face. That's how real women look, and that's what looks beautiful to me. I want to empower women of all ages, races, body types, and skin tones to feel and look like their authentic, beautiful selves.

Nothing was going to stop me from launching the brand on the day my noncompete expired. Everyone told me to wait. The world was a mess, and the 2020 presidential election was dominating everyone's attention, but I was determined. I agreed to one concession: October 24 was a Saturday, so we'd launch two days later on the 26th. As the launch date approached, we still didn't have a name. I couldn't use my name or any part of it. I asked friends to help, and we hired copywriters, who suggested names nobody liked. Naming a brand is like naming your kid. There's a lot of pressure, and you don't get a second chance.

Steven and I were driving in the Hamptons and he said, "If we don't pick a name by Monday, we'll have to delay the launch."

When he drives, Steven likes navigating with Waze and Google Maps and he's always in a hurry. I glanced at the map just as we were passing a random road called Jones Road. The name stuck in my head.

I said, "Jones Road Beauty."

"I like it," Steven said.

To me, it sounded like a bespoke British brand, and as an Anglophile, it was just the feel I wanted. Plus, I couldn't use Brown, so Jones seemed like a good option.

I texted the office and they all loved it. We called our lawyer, and it was available. Just like that, our new brand had a name: Jones Road.

One of my favorite parts in creating a brand is the visuals. We hired two cool downtown girls to create the logo, web design, and everything else we needed to launch. We had a photo shoot in our photo studio. I was nervous because we didn't want news to leak before the launch, and people still felt uneasy about being close together indoors. Taking precautions, we gathered for a test of concept. The photos were as wonderful as I envisioned and absolutely supported the looks we imagined. Jones Road was ready!

CHAPTER THIRTY-SEVEN

COMPETE

I wanted everything about Jones Road to be different. No corporate parent, no global teams, no investor demands, no department stores, no fancy packaging or displays. We would sell directly to the consumer. We would be small, scrappy, streamlined. We interviewed leading PR and marketing companies but I thought they were too conventional. I didn't want convention.

We engaged my friend and neighbor Lynette Brubaker, who had her own PR and marketing firm. We understood each other and she believed in me. She landed us a business story in *The Wall Street Journal* and got the *Today* show to air a seven-minute TV segment, which they filmed in our office. I also made an appearance, from my couch, on Elvis Duran's radio show, which had a huge audience. We mailed about 250 gift boxes to our FOBs (Friends of Bobbi): people of influence like Kris Jenner, Deborah Roberts, Cindy Crawford, and Padma Lakshmi.

On the morning of October 26, 2020, I went to the office and unlocked the Instagram account that my creative director and I had created . . . and we went live! I posted a story on my personal Instagram account, which had a few hundred thousand followers. Jones Road was open for business at 10:00 a.m.

I was nervous. I didn't know if anyone would like my new makeup. Maybe it wouldn't work. But I was also very excited. I believed in the product and thought others would also.

Thankfully, it didn't take long to find out. The response was immediate and overwhelming. People were excited, and the orders were flying in. We had produced enough Miracle Balm to last three months, or so we thought, but it sold out in three weeks. The department stores were contacting me asking to carry Jones Road. We got a great response on social media.

Bobbi Brown Cosmetics was sold in department stores, but the strategy was for Jones Road to be sold directly to consumers on our website. We control one hundred percent of the way the product was presented and marketed. I wanted Jones Road to be done my way.

We were scrappy and solved problems quickly and creatively. We sold out of Miracle Balm with hundreds of orders still pending. It would take several months to get it back in stock. We hadn't anticipated the demand, and the supply chain was nonexistent. There was nothing to do but wait. Then we got a call from the warehouse. They'd located twenty-five hundred Dusty Rose Miracle Balms in a corner, but they didn't have boxes. Those would take a month to reorder. "No way," I said. I had someone go to the grocery store, buy white paper sandwich bags and neon pink tape, and print the ingredients on a card that fit in the bag. We put up a post on our social media, sold all the balms in a day or two, and mailed them out in our makeshift packaging.

A year or so after that, we ran out of mascara. This also sold much faster than we had anticipated. We hadn't yet hired a demand planner—an expert who projects sales of products and manages inventory to meet expected demands. Chrissy told me that with our packaging, it would take many months to get the tubes to match. We had enough matte tops, but only shiny bottoms available. When we launched Bobbi Brown at Bergdorf Goodman in 1991, I almost had a nervous breakdown when I noticed that the lipstick tubes didn't match the lids. Now I realized that the product inside was much more important than the packaging. Even though the components didn't match, I said, "That's okay, do it." As a result, we were able to get mascara back in stock in weeks instead of months.

At Bobbi Brown Cosmetics, we'd plan product launches at least eighteen months ahead of release dates because of the required coordination with corporate approvals, the retailers, and manufacturers. With Jones Road, we shortened our lead time to eight months or less, mainly because we didn't have retailers to work with, and our manufactures were smaller and faster. By the end of 2020, the pandemic was getting under control, and Jones Road was even more successful than I had hoped. I wasn't surprised. I really believed in the project. I was relieved and elated. I felt reborn at sixty-two years old.

CHAPTER THIRTY-EIGHT

A FAMILY AFFAIR

Jones Road grew fast. We started with four employees and struggled to keep up. Every employee wore many hats. We had to. No matter their job title, each person helped with social media and everyone packed and sent out boxes, including me.

I am very focused on visual details. We were launching pink glosses, but when we were preparing the products to ship to editors, I realized the inside of the box looked bland. We hadn't thought about how the inside package should look. I looked around the room and spotted some branded Jones Road pink sticky pads. I grabbed one and wrote: "Think Pink, xx, Bobbi." It made the package more visually interesting. I signed about three hundred by hand, and when people posted pictures on social of the product with the stickies around them, they generated a lot of love at no cost.

By the end of our first year in business, we had sold many more products than we'd forecasted. Customers seemed to really appreciate our creations. At the beginning of 2021, Steven had completed a new brick building near the office. He had a small retail space and he asked, "Do you want to open a store?" I loved the freedom of selling the product digitally; we didn't have a retail team, a store designer, or makeup artists on staff. But, why not?

We designed and built the store ourselves the same way we created the George: by walking around the empty store and visualizing where everything should go. Steven asked, "Where do you want the makeup tables? Where do you want the sign? What size? What should it be made of?" His creative vision influenced everything, from the funky cinder block walls to the steel tables and the stone countertops. We had no grand plan. We just did it.

The look of the store emphasized the essence of the brand. It was a little rough, a little edgy, and authentically us. Steven had his employees build a marble top table on steel wheels to showcase the makeup. We positioned the products on the table on trays and they looked flat. We needed more height. Steven said, "I have a construction site around the corner. Go and get some concrete pavers." We laughed as we walked down the street carrying these heavy blocks. We placed them on the table and they looked perfect. The pavers became part of our look.

A few days before the store opening, we thought the walls looked bare. Crunched for time, I had our creative director print the favorite photos from our photo shoots. We taped them on the wall with Jones Road–printed masking tape. That also became part of our look. The Montclair store opened in November 2021, with a local newspaper article and a few Instagram posts. We envisioned being open only a few days a week. Almost immediately lines of people formed on the sidewalk, customers still wearing masks to enter the store, six people at a time. We quickly realized that many people want to see, touch, and experience Jones Road in person and stayed open six days a week.

Selling at a retail store is very different than selling products digitally. Since we had just one full-time makeup artist, office employees took turns helping out as we began hiring more artists. Jones Road is different from conventional makeup brands, both in feel and in results, so the learning curve for our artists was bumpy in the beginning. Many customers ended up looking greasy because the artists intuitively applied moisturizers first, followed by the uber-emollient What the Foundation, which made the face too shiny. When Miracle Balm was layered on top of all this, it was not a pretty look, nor was it what we intended. We had to train the artists before they could see customers.

At the end of 2021, we realized we were onto something—the growth was beyond our expectations. We needed help, especially in marketing, but no one on staff had the expertise. The beauty landscape had changed.

Then, unexpectedly, Cody appeared.

Cody had become an expert in digital marketing, helping Payal run their physical therapy business. He took independent courses on the subject and it became his passion. He was always in my ear telling me not to hire a normal ad agency when we started Jones Road.

Cody was happy to give advice as a consultant (he had run Evolution_18's growth), but he was still not interested in joining the family business. But his digital sales strategies began making a huge difference. He took over digital marketing and growth, then finally agreed to become a full-time employee. We were still a relatively small team, and his knowledge was a game changer. And Jones Road was growing fast. As Cody took a leadership role (which has continued to elevate as the company has grown), Payal was figuring out what she wanted to do after selling her business. Renovating houses and starting a food company were both on the table. She is extremely capable, and we begged her to help with our social media strategy. I have total confidence in her opinions and her ability to step in and understand what needs to be done.

Eventually, Payal agreed to be our head of brand. Dylan, Duke, and Kim all said a hard no when we asked them to come on board in some capacity, but they remain my go-to people for opinions on all things related to the business. As of this writing, Cody has become CEO and our first employee, Chrissy, is the COO.

In early 2021, Cody and I had a call with Gary Vaynerchuk, a brilliant digital-marketing businessman and a friend, for advice on content. Gary said: "Stop whatever you're doing, focus on Bobbi's personal TikTok, hire an agency or hire a team, but don't wait. Go deep, and go authentic."

The TikTok craze wasn't a thing yet. I stressed over the complexity of following Gary's advice and wasn't sure where to begin. Cody didn't hesitate; he pulled out his iPhone and said, "Mom, go."

Just like that, without makeup, without even looking in the mirror or thinking about what to say, I recorded a TikTok: "Hi, everyone, it's Bobbi. I'm new to TikTok. What do you want to know from me?"

That first video got more than three hundred thousand views and more than twenty-five hundred comments. I was shocked by how many people responded, "Help! How do I make myself look less tired?" I was surprised the audience was not all teenagers. "I'm over fifty and don't know what to do to look better." Neither Cody nor I knew the over-thirty audience was on TikTok. Our next focus was answering people's questions. I answered questions as Cody filmed, and he posted my responses. Some started to go viral, especially the ones that began, "If you're over fifty . . ." When I told my story about refusing a nose job, people shared it.

Gary was right.

Good news: sales multiplied.

Bad news: we soon ran out of stock of the products I mentioned in the videos.

We quickly realized social media was an important medium for the brand. To teach and not sell, as I did on the *Today* show and QVC. My role is to educate and answer questions. TikTok, unlike television, provides instant feedback. This isn't always a good thing. When a makeup influencer with a large following reviewed "What the Foundation," it was a near disaster. She took a big glop of it in each hand, rubbed it all over her face, and said she hated it. By the time her video came to my attention, it had thirteen million views—and thousands of comments agreeing with her.

I was crushed—and worried. I believed in the product, but I

know not everyone loves this style of makeup, or knows how to actually use it. I immediately went into our makeshift content studio and made several how-to videos.

In one video, I said, "If you favor full coverage and matte foundation, Jones Road isn't for you. But if you like fresh, no-makeup makeup, this is how you use it." I held up a small, finger-sized amount. When we were finished, I told my team, "I have one more to shoot." Then, to the camera, I said, "I always love learning new makeup techniques, and I learned one today." I took two big glops of What the Foundation, rubbed them on my face, and burst out laughing. I had no intention of posting it. It was just for comic relief. After we left the office, I told Duke what happened. He said, "Mom, don't put that up. You can't go against a huge TikTok influencer." I hung up and called Cody to tell him not to release the video.

"Too late, Mom," he said. "The train has left the station."

The video went viral. Viewers said, "Bobbi Brown clapped back" (a new term to me), meaning I wasn't afraid to challenge this influencer. I did it with humor. The comments were mostly positive and supportive of me and Jones Road. The interesting thing to me was how fast the press ran with the story. Overnight, there was global news about the incident and how some influencers can derail a brand's launch and how wrong that was. Fortunately for us, the incident had a very positive sales impact.

I didn't expect to become a TikTok star in my sixties, but then again, I also hadn't expected our sales growth to be so quick. We had a new problem: we couldn't keep products in stock. If something became unavailable, I'd make another video, saying, "We're so glad you like it. I promise we're going to get it back. If you want to add your name to the waitlist, go to the website." In that way, we gathered names and emails of new customers and continued to grow the business.

At this point, it was time to focus inwardly on the business structure. Our operations team had to support the health of the business and make decisions on forecasting and ordering. I needed to rely on others to do this and tell me it was being handled. My first employee, Chrissy, whom I hired to do product development, became more involved and began overseeing operations. She implemented smart, simple procedures, like ordering enormous amounts of empty packaging to store so we would be ready to fill orders much faster. She is now our COO. It took Cody and me a while to learn how to work effectively together. At first he would quit every few days. We often discuss if he works for me or if I work for him. It's amazing for me to sit in meetings and watch my kid be so brilliant. I heard him say his first words; now he's talking about things I don't understand. I'm beyond proud of him.

There are, of course, cons to working with family. Often, there's no separation between work and home. Most of our conversations include products, people, strategies, and sales. It's sometimes a struggle for Cody and me to turn it off and just be mother and son.

I can say things to Cody I wouldn't say to anyone else. We are often blunt and open with each other. This has actually been an unexpected blessing. It has caused me to listen, and grow in ways I probably wouldn't have.

Cody has an ability to give me constructive criticism. After a meeting he'll often say, "Mom, are you open to some feedback?" At first I'd bristle at the suggestion. You're telling me I did something wrong?! But because he's my son, I calm down and listen. Sometimes he's right. He'll say, "Today in the meeting, you didn't let someone finish talking," or "Today in the meeting, it seemed like your ideas were more important than everyone else's." Who tells their boss this stuff? But because he's my kid I listen.

Cody understands what they call "Bobbi-speak." He has become my translator. I'll send an email with vague, half-finished sentences, that I think is clear, and he'll respond to the team: "This is what Bobbi means."

Proud, grateful, optimistic, relaxed, and way more grounded is how I see myself the second time around. Problems, issues, and aggravations are part of business and, frankly, part of life. But the stress I felt at Estée Lauder is very different from the stress I experience today. Fortunately, I handle it differently. I am better at knowing what I can and cannot control. I am surrounded by people I adore—my family and colleagues who have become like family. I'm better able to handle it this time around.

Now, five years into Jones Road, we have a successful, profitable business. I'm not sure what the future will bring, but I am very happy and am enjoying the journey.

CHAPTER THIRTY-NINE

I AM ME

I've always believed that aging is beautiful. And that being natural is beautiful. Who we are, the years we earn—these are not things to fight or fix. My mission, throughout my career and life, has been to empower women to define themselves on their own terms. To encourage them to never let society's standards dictate what they should look like, how they should age, or who they should be.

But it's one thing to believe something—and another to build something around it. I didn't just want to say it. I wanted to show it. That's how the I Am Me initiative at Jones Road was born: as a way to turn this philosophy into something you could see, hear, and feel. Something that could live beyond me.

We created I Am Me at Jones Road to do just that—to inspire confidence through storytelling. These weren't marketing stories. They were real conversations, told without filters, about the beauty standards women have endured for decades and the impact these have had on women's self-esteem. Some of what was shared was deeply personal. All of it was powerful.

The very first I Am Me gathering was a sleepover and beauty party at the George Hotel. Thirty incredible women I admire showed up—actresses, activists, supermodels, journalists, entrepreneurs, and more. The intention was simple: start conversations that could help us build a healthier perspective on beauty and aging. Conversations that could ripple outward to future generations.

What happened in that room was unforgettable.

An actress shared that she'd been told—more than once—that she should get surgery to "fix" her nose. A former supermodel revealed that, in her prime, she was told to eat cotton balls so she wouldn't feel hungry. Others opened up about long histories with eating disorders. One woman told us her agent had advised her to lose fifteen pounds and have two ribs removed.

That night, the beauty industry's old rules were laid bare. And we weren't afraid to say them out loud.

One of my favorite moments came from a journalist—smart, successful, grounded—who said, "If we want to change the narrative around aging, we can't just say it's cool. We have to make it cool. We have to live it." She talked about the joy of looking in the mirror at 50 or 60 and seeing not flaws, but confidence. Not "used to be," but "still becoming." She's doing exactly that—and showing other women how.

The conversations shifted to women in TV and film, and the difficulty of aging in public. We talked about what it means to stop apologizing for who we are, to let go of outside pressure, and quiet the noise in our own heads. There was laughter. There were tears. There was real forward-thinking about how to change the culture—not just for ourselves, but for the next generation.

We ended the afternoon with a charged, unforgettable discussion led by activist Gloria Steinem. We talked about confidence, empowerment, and what it was like for her to lead the women's movement—what's changed, and what still needs to.

Athletes, founders, influencers, artists—women from their twenties to their nineties—were all there. We spanned every decade, and every voice added something essential. I don't think I could ever replicate the experience. It was lightning in a bottle.

But I knew we had to try.

The challenge became: How do we take this intimate, emotional, transformative gathering and share it with more than just 30 women? I asked my team to put together a deck. We started pitching. We talked to everyone we could think of—brands, media partners, sponsors—hoping someone would see the vision.

It took months. There were setbacks. There were moments I was ready to give up. I needed the right partner.

And then, after nearly nine months, J.P. Morgan Chase came through. They understood what we were trying to build. They believed in the mission. And they agreed to support a new I Am Me series—one that we would shoot right in Montclair, in our Jones Road content studio.

Today, I Am Me is a ten-episode video series available on YouTube and shared across our social channels. The content is honest, bold, and, I hope, transformative. It's about confidence. It's about self-expression through beauty. And it's about financial independence—because that's part of the conversation too.

We talk about the challenges these women faced, and how they overcame them. It's real, it's vulnerable, and it's strong.

I'm incredibly proud of the work. And more than that, I hope it lives on—far beyond the videos. I hope it gives other women permission to stand taller, speak louder, age proudly, and say, "I am me."

CHAPTER FORTY

THE GLUE

A life isn't something you inherit. It's something you assemble.

You find the pieces, sometimes carefully, sometimes by accident—and you start building. A moment here. A friend there. A good idea. A risk that pays off. A trip that resets your perspective. Slowly, these pieces become something whole. Soon you realize, I am me! These pieces make me who I am.

Family is the glue. Not just the origin story—but the ongoing structure. They are the steady hands that hold me up when I need the support. And just like the best glue, they've stretched and expanded with time. Sisters. In-laws. Nieces. Nephews. Cousins. Partners of cousins. New babies. We keep making room, and somehow it all still fits. Stronger and tighter than ever.

And then there are the people you choose to be in your family. The Montclair friends are family. There are others we met through travel, work, or sheer luck. I am grateful to have met a lot of wonderful people. It's been an honor to bring our friends into the family.

My work life has been one of my greatest creative projects—and one of my greatest sources of loss. Leaving Bobbi Brown Cosmetics meant losing a team that felt like an extension of me—people I got to bounce ideas off of and with whom I got to work on exciting projects. I depended on them for support, and remain grateful for that support. Starting over taught me something crucial: you can build again.

The new team I've created brings energy and ideas that keep me sharp. Keeps me young, even. They are collaborators, co-conspirators, and constant sources of laughter. They remind me how much I still love the work.

And then there's the joy I never saw coming—being a grandmother. Lily, and now Shaan, have redefined what matters. With them, time slows down. When Lily says "Only BB," it's not a request. It's a spell. In that moment, everything else falls away. She shows up on set and wants to be held while she applies makeup and selects jewelry for the models. She's confident, decisive, unbothered by the production schedule. It's my favorite kind of chaos. And yes, my weight training helps when I have to pick her up.

I've always been the one doing the crafting. Gluing—curating, connecting, combining the pieces into a life meaningful to me. But it's my family, in every form, that holds the whole thing together when it matters. They keep the edges from curling. They make the pieces fit.

A life, after all, is what you make it.

CHAPTER FORTY-ONE

MY LUNCH WITH LEONARD

On Leonard Lauder's ninetieth birthday I sent him an email. I hadn't spoken to him since I left the brand six years before. It was March 2023. My message was short and sweet. I wanted him to know how much he meant to me.

He quickly replied with an invitation to lunch at his apartment.

More than thirty years had passed since my first meal with Leonard. In 1997 I was a thirty-four-year-old new mom with a growing business, on the cusp of a life I could barely imagine. Now I had three grown children, two grandchildren, and in my mid-sixties, had built a large cosmetic brand, and had started building another.

I was nervous. I hadn't seen him in years. I didn't know what to expect. I remembered the same feelings before first meeting him all those years earlier.

Leonard was as wonderful, loving, complimentary, honest, and open as always. We spent three hours together, looking out over the park, eating and reminiscing. We talked about the people we knew, the ones we loved and the ones we didn't. I told him exactly what I felt and how much I loved and respected him. He did the same. The rest of that conversation will remain unsaid.

He asked about Jones Road, and I told him how well it was going. We had just opened another store in Greenwich Village, and we were about to open one in East Hampton (over the next year, Palm Beach, Chicago, and Brooklyn would join the roster with Austin and Boston on deck). He was happy for me.

Leonard hugged me goodbye. Then he said, "I'm sorry."

This threw me. This man had helped make my wildest dreams come true. What could he possibly be sorry for?

"For what?" I asked.

"I promised I would take care of you and the brand," he said, "and I wasn't able to do that."

I looked him in the eye.

"Leonard," I said, "I'm so grateful it happened exactly the way it happened. I promise you, I wouldn't change a thing."

A SPECIAL EDITION OF **WWD**

BEAUTY INC

THE
PETE BORN
IMPACT AWARD

Road
Warrior

HOW **BOBBI BROWN** CHANGED THE FACE
OF BEAUTY NOT JUST ONCE — BUT TWICE

FULL CIRCLE

As I was finishing this book, I got a call from *Women's Wear Daily*. They wanted to honor me with their prestigious Impact Award. I'm not big on receiving awards but this one is the fashion equivalent of a lifetime achievement Oscar, and it was an honor to accept it.

The award ceremony was held December 2024 in Manhattan's Rainbow Room, sixty-five floors above the holiday crowds and the bustle and where I had arrived as a wide-eyed girl forty years earlier. The dining room was packed with hundreds of people—a who's who of the beauty industry.

I climbed to the stage and stood at the microphone as a video summarizing my career played on the large screen behind me. I looked around the room; I smiled seeing colleagues, family, and friends at my table. At another table sat Estée Lauder executives, including William Lauder.

Sprinkled around the room I saw the faces of many former Bobbi Brown employees who had continued their careers with new founders and new brands. Some as CEOs. I felt like a proud mama. I was a little overwhelmed.

I caught a glimpse of my husband, tears in his eyes looking at me. I felt the love from the room; it was an out-of-body experience. I thought I was dreaming.

I remembered the teenager in suburban Chicago who hadn't yet seen Ali MacGraw in *Love Story* and who felt overshadowed by her mother's glamour. I thought about the young girl who tried to find a college that would teach her about makeup and how fortunate she was that she knew someone who knew someone who suggested Emerson. I thought about the determined, naive, and lucky young woman who showed up at the makeup union office in New York City. Could any of those girls have imagined what they could possibly accomplish? Could any of these younger Bobbis ever have imagined walking across the stage to receive a lifetime beauty achievement award? Could any have imagined having an adoring family, supportive colleagues, and a makeup career that continues to engage and challenge her?

I wanted to go back in time and tell those younger Bobbis, and all girls, to stay true to themselves, and their vision, and their belief in real beauty, and to know that things will work out. Trust me. They really will.

And then I realized—I don't have to tell that girl anything. She is me. I am her. And after all these years, I'm still Bobbi.

All in all, it's been a great ride. And so cathartic to have written this memoir. What have I learned that I didn't know? That this is who I am, and this might be why I am the way I am. And I'm okay. It's okay!

All my love—
BOBBI

ACKNOWLEDGMENTS

This journey has been cathartic. I highly recommend the process of writing your life story, even if it's only written for the next generation. I have many people I'm grateful for and want to thank.

My agent Rebecca Gradinger of UTA, who showed up at my office one afternoon and somehow convinced me I had a story to tell, your persistent encouragement got me here. You are not only my agent; you are my friend.

Travis, my writer who listened, asked the difficult questions, and visualized the themes as I began to explore my past, our talks while I walked were enjoyable and enlightening. (And my Oura Ring was happy with the step count.)

My publisher, Marysue Rucci, who—from the first meeting— had so much belief in me and enthusiasm for the project, helped shape the words throughout the story. Thank you to the entire Simon & Schuster team for your constant support.

To my amazing UK team—my agent, Felicity Blunt at Curtis

Brown, and my editors at Bloomsbury, Ian Marshall and Jasmine Horsley—thanks to each of you and your teams for your determination in bringing this book to life across the pond. And thank you to my UK PR agency, Blanket PR, for your enthusiasm and hard work.

Lynette, my rock star Manager/PR Agent/Friend, you make everything look so easy. I don't know how you do it, but I'm so glad you do.

Erin, my creative director at Jones Road, your eye, your instinct, your vibe. I'm lucky to work with you.

Gianna and Courtney, my A team, thank you for juggling the chaos, keeping things on track, decoding my handwriting, and doing it all with a great attitude. I'd be lost without you.

Cheyenne, for more than just makeup—thank you for everything you do.

Ben Ritter, thank you for your ease and beautiful photography.

And of course, my friends who gave me great edits and advice.

Lastly, to my boys, Steven (my biggest editor and champion); sons Dylan, Cody, and Duke; daughters-in-law Kim and Payal, for being my sounding board, my calm, and my heart. You've been through all of it with me, and I couldn't love you more.

This was a team effort. Thank you with all my heart.

Bobbi

PHOTO GLOSSARY

ENDPAPERS

1. Women of Influence Event in Montclair, NJ
Courtesy of: Bobbi Brown's Personal Archive

2. Jones Road Beauty Photo Shoot
Photo by: Ben Ritter

3. Jeopardy Question "Who is Bobbi Brown"
Courtesy of: Bobbi Brown's Personal Archive

4. Italian *Vogue*: Carla Bruni
Printed with permission: Walter Chin

5. Bobbi and Parents Joe and Sandra
Courtesy of: Bobbi Brown's Personal Archive

6. Bobbi's Parents: Joe and Sandra
Courtesy of: Bobbi Brown's Personal Archive

7. Bobbi on Set
Photo by: Ben Ritter

8. Jones Road Beauty Miracle Balm
Photo by: Jon Paterson

9. Cody, Steven, Bobbi Brown, Dylan on Lake Michigan
Courtesy of: Jeff Licata

10. Bobbi Brown First 10 Lipstick Shades
Courtesy of: Bobbi Brown's Personal Archive

11. Bobbi Brown at Bergdorf Goodman
Courtesy of: Bobbi Brown's Personal Archive

12. Iris Apfel and Bobbi Brown
Photo by: Bruce Weber

13. Bobbi Brown and Oprah Winfrey on *The Oprah Winfrey Show*
Courtesy of: Bobbi Brown's Personal Archive

14. Bobbi and Sister Linda Arrandt
Courtesy of: Bobbi Brown's Personal Archive

15. Bobbi Brown and Yao Ming
Courtesy of: Bobbi Brown's Personal Archive

16. Quote by Aunt Alice
Courtesy of: Bobbi Brown's Personal Archive

Chapter 4: Know Where You're From—Bobbi and Her Parents
Courtesy of: Bobbi Brown's Personal Archive

Part 2: Know Who You Are—Bobbi as a Teenager
Courtesy of: Bobbi Brown's Personal Archive

Chapter 5: Real Faces—Ali MacGraw
Photo by: Getty Images

Chapter 6: Makeup University—Bobbi's First Fashion Show for Ford's Model of the Year Event.
Courtesy of: Bobbi Brown's Personal Archive

Part 3: Figure It Out—Bobbi on Caribbean Photo Shoot Tour
Courtesy of: Bobbi Brown's Personal Archive

Chapter 7: Go See—Bobbi's First Business Card
Courtesy of: Bobbi Brown's Personal Archive

Chapter 8: Glitz and Glamour—*Cosmopolitan* Cover Featuring Jerry Hall
Permission from: Douglas Dubler

Chapter 9: Climb the Ladder—Tatjana Patitz / Makeup by Bobbi
Permission from: Wayne Maser

Chapter 10: One Door Closes—Bobbi and Steven's Wedding
Courtesy of: Bobbi Brown's Personal Archive

Chapter 11: Cover Girl 1989—September 1989 *Vogue* Cover
Courtesy of: Patrick Demarchelier / Trunk Archive

Part 4: What if/ Why Not—Bobbi In MTC Home Office
Courtesy of: Bobbi Brown's Personal Archive

Chapter 12: The Burbs—Steven Reading *NJ LIFE* Magazine
Courtesy of: Bobbi Brown's Personal Archive

Chapter 13: Reinventing Lipstick—Bobbi's Original 10 Lipstick Shades
Courtesy of: Bobbi Brown's Personal Archive

Chapter 14: Working Mom—Baby Dylan with Supermodel
Courtesy of: Bobbi Brown's Personal Archive

Chapter 15: The Brand—Bobbi and Family Outside Bergdorf Goodman
Courtesy of: Bobbi Brown's Personal Archive

Chapter 16: Essentials—Bobbi Brown Essentials Launch Invitation
Courtesy of: Bobbi Brown's Personal Archive

Chapter 17: Work/Life Balance—Bobbi and Sons Dylan and Cody
Courtesy of: Bobbi Brown's Personal Archive

Chapter 18: What If/Why Not—Billboard-Dallas TX + Bobbi and Cody on Lake Michigan
Photo by: Jeffrey Licata

Part 5: Be Normal—Bobbi, Brie Larson, and Meryl Streep
Courtesy of: Bobbi Brown's Personal Archive

Chapter 19: On Top of the World—Bobbi and Leonard Lauder
Courtesy of: Bobbi Brown's Personal Archive

Chapter 20: The Wonder Years—Bobbi in *Forbes*
Courtesy of: Bobbi Brown's Personal Archive

Chapter 21: The Glory Years—Bobbi at the Met Gala
Courtesy of: Bobbi Brown's Personal Archive

Chapter 22: Downtown Bobbi Brown—NYC Office
Courtesy of: Bobbi Brown's Personal Archive